THE
APOSTOLIC
FATHERS

Abingdon Essential Guides

The Bible in English Translation
Steven M. Sheeley and Robert N. Nash, Jr.

Christian Ethics
Robin W. Lovin

Church History
Justo L. González

Feminism and Christianity
Lynn Japinga

Mission
Carlos F. Cardoza-Orlandi

Pastoral Care
John Patton

Preaching
Ronald J. Allen

Rabbinic Literature
Jacob Neusner

Worship in Ancient Israel
Walter Brueggemann

THE APOSTOLIC FATHERS
An
ESSENTIAL GUIDE

Clayton N. Jefford

Abingdon Press
Nashville

APOSTOLIC FATHERS
AN ESSENTIAL GUIDE

Copyright © 2005 by Abingdon Press

This book is printed on acid-free paper.

Library of Congress Cataloging-in-Publication Data

Jefford, Clayton N.
   The Apostolic Fathers : an essential guide / Clayton N. Jefford.
      p. cm.
   Includes bibliographical references.
   ISBN 0-687-34204-X (pbk. : alk. paper)
 1. Apostolic Fathers.   I. Title.

   BR67.J44 2005
   270.1—dc22

                                                                2005017895

05 06 07 08 09 10 11 12 13 14—10 9 8 7 6 5 4 3 2 1

MANUFACTURED IN THE UNITED STATES OF AMERICA

Contents

Introduction

The present volume is intended to offer a simple and sensible approach to a small collection of early Christian writings that scholars of church history commonly call the Apostolic Fathers. A broad range of texts is included within this unique collection. For example, there are several letters to be found here, witnesses to the immediate thoughts and concerns of extraordinary people who shaped the development of early Christianity as a faith. One also discovers theological tractates, some of which were probably offered as homilies, or sermons, and others of which were constructed to guide the earliest believers in route to an appropriate ethical lifestyle and along their path toward personal spiritual development. So too, our collected works include a witness to the martyrdom of a renowned bishop, an apologetic defense of the church's right to exist in the world, and the gathering of sayings, parables, and random teachings from the traditions of some of Christianity's most original authors.

The materials that appear within the Apostolic Fathers form a witness to the historical transition that the early church made from its New Testament roots to the later patristic period. They offer the details of ancient Christianity as it struggled to develop into an organization that eventually transcended its origins as a loose confederation of independent church communities, most of which met to worship and share their faith experiences within the homes of individual believers. And yet, what remains here is the perspective of a people who did not yet have access to the broad and tightly knit standards that the later institutional church was to offer for subsequent preachers, teachers, and theologians. In other words, the Apostolic Fathers preserve a narrow historical moment in the life of the early church. The voices of their authors attest to the rise of a faith consciousness among Christians who were widely scattered around the ancient Mediterranean world. Each of them offered a special sense of what it meant to follow Jesus of Nazareth as the Messiah in their day. And each of them proffers a unique insight into what it should mean for us to be people of faith in a postmodern world.

In the pages that follow, the reader will hopefully find a helpful presentation of the most important themes and issues that the Apostolic Fathers have to offer for our comprehension of Christian tradition. A variety of topics will be addressed throughout the volume, each of which is offered as a single spoke in a revolving wheel of approaches to the authors who lie behind our writings, the audiences to whom they wrote, and the issues to which they devoted their lives.

The initial chapter presents a brief overview of the basic information that is necessary to appreciate the individual writings within the Apostolic Fathers. After an opening explanation of the origins of the collection, the individual texts will be addressed in rough chronological order. The reader will find some clarification behind the questions of authorship, date, and the intended audience for each work, the circumstances under which the texts were written, and the themes that are typical of each author and that make each writing unique within the collection.

The second chapter is devoted to those important leaders of the early church who have provided us with the literature we have today. Their lives of faith, their theological speculation, their relationships with one another, and their experience with the risen Christ have all been preserved for us in the writings they have left behind. This chapter provides a brief glimpse into the historical and geographical settings in which these early thinkers labored. As we might expect, our understanding of the context in which they wrote helps us better to appreciate the meaning that they intended as they worked.

The pages following these two opening chapters present a variety of issues that will help us to realize the unique role of the Apostolic Fathers within the development of the early church, as well as their place in Christian literature. It is hoped that the presentation of such themes and ideas will enable the reader to place each text within a broader sphere of influences within the ancient church. Indeed, in order to appreciate the Apostolic Fathers, both as literature and as a witness to the earliest faith of post-apostolic Christianity, it is necessary to envision the world in which those texts were produced.

We will begin with a discussion of the importance of scripture within the rise of the early Christian consciousness. In that process we will define the role that the authoritative texts of ancient Judaism held for the first Christians. The prominence of holy writings and sacred traditions within the early church is easily detected throughout the writings of our collection.

After our discussion of the significance of scripture, we will survey the most important theological ideas that are preserved within the Apostolic Fathers. Many of these foundational insights came to form the background of issues and debates that have pushed theologians and church historians into a clearer understanding of what it means to be a Christian . . . even until today. As a church community we too often skip back over the history of Christianity's development and evolution to focus our interest upon the scriptures alone. With the Apostolic Fathers we can begin to understand how the world of the Bible influenced later church history and brought us to the present.

We will then examine the foundational structure of the church from its existence in the late first and early second centuries as revealed by our authors. It is presumed that the reader will come to see that the institutional models that most Christians now consider to be normative, particularly in Western culture, have been highly molded by the ideas that our writings first endorsed. This certainly holds true for the role of sacraments and for how we observe sacramental moments in the liturgical life of the church. Ancient ecclesiastical structure has also influenced the systems that we now employ to organize the leadership positions and functions of our denominations. And the standards we typically endorse as "an appropriate lifestyle" for being a faithful follower of the teachings of God clearly have their roots in our literature.

Finally, we will review the impact the Apostolic Fathers had upon the immediate generation of Christians that followed in their wake. These believers in the risen Christ, who lived from the late second through the sixth centuries, ultimately provided a framework for subsequent Christian theology as practiced by the church today. What we discover is that the foundational judgments of the great theologians from the patristic period were molded as much by our authors as by the pedigree of scripture that stands at the origin of the church's faith.

Where to Find the Texts in Translation

Because the materials that appear here are designed to introduce the reader to a very specific collection of texts in the most efficient and helpful way possible within the confines of a single, slim and manageable volume, there leaves no room to provide the writings of the Apostolic Fathers themselves. Some readers undoubtedly will be satisfied merely to read *about* these texts, but many others will wish to explore the works directly. At the moment the entire corpus of the collection is available in two publications of good, solid English translation:

Ehrman, Bart D., ed. and trans. *The Apostolic Fathers.* 2 vols. Loeb Classical Library 24-25. Cambridge, Mass. & London: Harvard University Press, 2003.

Holmes, Michael W., ed. and trans. *The Apostolic Fathers.* Revised edition. Grand Rapids, Mich.: Baker Books, 1999.

There is yet another older translation of the collected works that is fairly inexpensive and very popular among students. Unfortunately, it omits several longer writings in the collection:

Louth, Andrew, ed. *Early Christian Writings: The Apostolic Fathers.* Revised edition. Maxwell Staniforth, trans. New York: Penguin Books, 1987.

CHAPTER 1

The Collected Writings

T he anthology of writings that we now call the Apostolic Fathers was not recognized as a unified set of texts within the early church. Much like the works that came to form our New Testament, the several letters and tractates that have been preserved in our collection circulated individually among early Christian communities where they were gathered together and used for inspiration, teaching, liturgy, and other reasons that are now lost to us. We are left, then, to explore how and why these particular texts eventually came to be placed together within a single collection.

In large part our Apostolic Fathers represent the remnants of early Christian writings that ultimately did not make it into the New Testament canon. The formation of the Christian Bible, including materials that now appear either in the Old Testament, New Testament, or Apocrypha, was certainly the product of a long and complicated history. For the moment let us simply say that there was a clear concern among second- and third-generation Christians to assemble a collection of writings that could be generally acknowledged as authoritative in matters of faith, ethics, and theology. The materials that ultimately became the Hebrew Bible of rabbinic Judaism naturally were used from the very beginning of Christianity and were considered to be a valid reflection of

God's interaction with humanity. This was true for the most part because the first Christians arose from within Judaism, sharing the cultural values of the synagogue and its concern for divine laws and cultic rituals.

At the same time, however, those who came to confess a belief in Jesus of Nazareth as the Messiah found that their own writings also carried certain weight as confessional documents that were useful for instruction and worship. Early churches soon collected such "Christian" literary witnesses, cherishing their value as a testimony to the life of faith that existed among the churches and appreciating the normative standard that such documents offered for Christians as they traveled from one geographical region to another. But the process by which texts were chosen for preservation was not always well defined.

Thus, for example, the early second-century teacher Marcion of Sinope in Asia Minor made a concerted effort to gather copies of letters by the apostle Paul (Marcion's personal faith hero) and, placing them together with the Gospel of Luke, fashioned a sort of unofficial canon of authoritative writings. This feat reflected a natural tendency of the period. Unfortunately, not all Christians shared in the reasoning behind Marcion's actions, since he falsely attributed to Paul the belief that the God of Christianity was different from that deity who both appeared and acted under the name of "God" in the Old Testament. In essence, Marcion rejected the role of Judaism and its scriptures as an essential part of salvation history.

It was partially in response to the efforts of theologians like Marcion that other Christians began to gather additional texts into a usable collection that could be employed with confidence among the churches. Over a period of years a loose set of guidelines developed by which writings could be judged as suitable for use among the churches. These guidelines included principles that were related to theological suitability, broad usage among different congregations, connection with a valid apostolic witness, liturgical usefulness, and so forth. Of course, the wide expansion of early Christianity led to numerous efforts and varying results, including the incorporation of selected gospel works, letters from apostles and evangelists, collections of sayings that were attributed either to the historical Jesus or to revelations of the risen

Christ, memoirs of the acts of the first missionaries, theological tractates, and other literary genres. The debate over which of these writings were suitable for the extended church continued for several centuries and remains even today as a minor disagreement among the primary Christian denominations of the world, that is, Protestant, Roman Catholic, and Greek Orthodox.

At the same time, it is clear that some uniformity of texts had begun to gain recognition toward the end of the fourth century. This is demonstrated in the famous Festal Letter 39 by Bishop Athanasius of Alexandria, Egypt, a missive that the bishop sent to Christians of his diocese in 367 C.E. in order to indicate the appropriate date for the observance of Easter in that year. In his letter the bishop cataloged all those texts that he considered to bear the weight of canonical authority, a listing that includes today's Old Testament (except for the book of Esther) and New Testament. In addition, he offered several other writings that, while not considered to be canonical, were worthy of use for instruction. Featured here is the book of Esther, several works of the modern Apocrypha, and two writings that now are included among the Apostolic Fathers, the *Didache* and the *Shepherd of Hermas*.

What we learn about the Apostolic Fathers from this effort of the church to establish a canon of authoritative scriptures is at least twofold. In the first place, while the writings that are now included in our collection were not ultimately chosen to form a portion of the sacred canon of scripture, they likewise were not considered to be scandalous or "heretical" with respect to the theological mainstream of the evolving institutional church. This is significant because it means that later church authorities felt free to use these texts and the ideas of their authors as they made theological decisions and developed positions on an ethical Christian lifestyle. And secondly, for some Christians at least, a few of the texts that came to form the Apostolic Fathers were viewed with a reverence that may have approached that of scripture. This is suggested by the fact that some of our writings were included alongside New Testament literature in ancient, revered versions of the Bible. Thus, the fourth-century *Codex Sinaiticus*, an important early version of the New Testament, concludes with the texts of *Barnabas* and the *Shepherd of Hermas*, while the fifth-century *Codex Alexandrinus* concludes with the works of *1–2 Clement*. The importance of this observation should not be underestimated, since the appearance of at least some of our writings among the collected sacred texts of the ancient church suggests that they too were held in very high esteem. Indeed, their value for our understanding of early Christianity and its traditions should not be swept aside because of our own ignorance either of their content or of their relevance to other early church authors.

The phrase "apostolic fathers" appears to have been used rarely in early Christian literature prior to the medieval period. Even then, it is never applied to any single, specific collection of texts. Instead, the phrase typically designated the teachings of certain authors who wrote prior to the later patristic period, the time of the great apologists, heresiologists, and theologians who dominated the first six centuries of church development.

The first "modern" usage of the phrase appears in the work of the French scholar Jean Cotelier, who issued a two-volume collection of writings by authors he believed "flourished during the apostolic times" (published in 1672). He specified that these authors either were friends or disciples of the apostles of Jesus, including the apostle Paul. Under this rubric, he chose to include a variety of works that were associated by title with the missionary Barnabas (known from Acts), the bishop Clement of Rome, the bishop Ignatius of Antioch in Syria, and the bishop Polycarp of Smyrna in Asia Minor. Each of these writings still appears in current versions of the Apostolic Fathers. But since the time of Cotelier, modern scholars have dropped his insistence that the authors of the Apostolic Fathers were necessarily "companions or disciples of the apostles." They focus instead upon the early nature of texts as an important criterion by which to include certain writings. The result of this change in orientation is that many other writings that Cotelier chose to include in the collection have been removed, primarily because they are now dated to a later period in the history of Christian literature. At the same time, several texts have been added that Cotelier either did not know or chose to omit.

It is now sufficient to say that those works that remain in the collection of the Apostolic Fathers are considered to be consistent with the general principles and theologies of an apostolic tradition that circulated among the churches from the end of the first century into the middle of the second century. These texts, only tentatively defined, are generally seen to include the following works: *Epistle of Barnabas, 1–2 Clement, Didache, Epistle to Diognetus, Epistles of Ignatius, Epistle of Polycarp, Martyrdom of Polycarp, Shepherd of Hermas*, and the fragments of Papias. As a collection, the Apostolic Fathers have no official ecclesiastical sanction or authority. The assemblage of such writings is purely a secondary process of modern scholarship. And yet, as a combined voice they speak loudly about the origins of early Christian faith and culture.

1. Epistle of Barnabas

The text of *Barnabas* offers an intriguing glimpse into the vitriolic debate that often characterized early Christianity's struggle with its Jewish heritage. Now divided into twenty-one chapters by modern scholars, the work is typically viewed as the compilation of two primary sections: a main argument in which the author explains how Christianity has inherited the divine covenant that Judaism had forsaken (chapters 1–17) and a secondary collection of teachings drawn from a literary tradition known as the "two ways" (chapters 18–21).

There is little that we can know with certainty about the origins of the writing. Most scholars believe that the ascription of the work to Barnabas, presumably the same missionary companion of Paul that we recognize from the New Testament,[1] is not authentic, but represents early Christian efforts to gain apostolic authority for the text in debates about its canonical value. *Barnabas* itself provides few clues with respect to the character of the author. The focus of the main argument is directed toward an exaltation of Christianity at the expense of Jewish tradition, emphasizing that the covenant that God once offered to the Jews has now been handed over to those who believe that the Messiah of Israel has come in the person of Jesus of Nazareth. On the surface, the hostile terminology employed in this claim may suggest that our author was a non-Jew who wished to wrestle Judaism's glory away from its moorings. At the same time, however, the careful way in which our author has made extended use of the Old Testament, both with respect to its writings and imagery, may

9

argue more forcefully on behalf of our author's status as a "true believer," perhaps a recent Jewish convert to the Christian faith.

It is extremely difficult to place the work within a specific geographical location during any particular period of time. Suggestions for a setting have traditionally ranged from Asia Minor to Syria, and from Palestine to Egypt. The most commonly accepted view is that our author was writing from Alexandria in Egypt. With respect to date, *Barnabas* was composed with some knowledge of the destruction of the Temple in Jerusalem in 70 C.E., but its author seems unaware of the construction of a Roman temple on the same site under the emperor Hadrian a generation later (135 C.E.). This might provide a general range of some sixty years for the work (70–135 C.E.), but there is little to suggest a more specific point in time.

The original circumstances of *Barnabas* have been widely debated. Though identified by its title as an "epistle," it has more the look of a theological tractate or, perhaps, a homily. The brief letter elements of the text include opening greetings and a thanksgiving as well as concluding blessings, but these are the only indication that the work was ever a letter. And these traits may actually represent a secondary alteration of the text. The core of the writing is an extended argument that carefully draws upon Jewish scriptures and traditions as it illustrates the numerous ways in which God's covenant has been transferred to Christians. Scholars have sometimes suggested that our author's knowledge of quite specific Old Testament materials may indicate the use of "testimonia," or scripture references that were collected around a single theme for use in liturgical readings, devotional reflection, or theological speculation by early Christians.

Our author is concerned about three primary doctrines of thought that fulfill all Christian knowledge: hope that provides faith, righteousness that fulfills judgment, and love that reflects the joy of righteous living. The materials that follow are a continuous comment upon these principles, lavishly illustrated by renowned figures and events from scripture. As our author states, it is necessary for Christians to receive God's covenant of grace in a deserving spirit. There is no time for delay in this process since there is a great urgency for action with respect to the divine timetable for salvation. With the cross of Jesus Christ and the destruction of the Jewish Temple in Jerusalem, all necessary signs of God's activity are now in place. The audience is encouraged to reach out for the eternal reward that has been offered through the new covenant and to live in a manner that is befitting of those who have rejected evil ways and who now seek to keep God's commandments. It is indeed a new culture of faith that our author has envisioned for the church.

2. First Clement

Unlike the text of *Barnabas*, it is clear that *1 Clement* was originally penned as a letter. Although unusually long for such a task (having been divided into sixty-five chapters), its primary goal is to address the problems of a specific community. The text itself indicates that *1 Clement* was offered by the church of Rome as a response to the situation of the church in Corinth, which had found itself in the midst of a struggle over ecclesiastical leadership. It seems that the older and respected leaders of the Corinthian faith community had been removed from office by the machinations of younger upstarts. The troublesome aspect of this transition had led some within the Corinthian church to write to Rome in an effort to remedy the situation.

Our text received its name early in the historical tradition under the assumption of later Christian writers that its author was Clement of Rome, who ultimately became a prominent bishop within the Roman church. In reality, the text makes no mention of Clement as its author and offers no appeal to any particular ecclesiastical authority. This has led certain scholars to speculate whether our author wrote from a particular vantage point that did not reflect the broader perspective of the church in Rome or, perhaps, did not have the ecclesiastical rank that would have been necessary to gain broad church approval for what is contained in the writing. It is sufficient to note for the present that tradition has assigned authorship to the figure of Clement, an important person who is known to have been a leader of the Roman church in the last half of the first century.

This raises the question of the letter's date of composition. Our author indicates that, like the Corinthians, the church in Rome had recently suffered through some troublesome times. Although it remains unclear whether this difficulty had come from outside the community or, instead, from within its ranks, scholars have traditionally been led to place *1 Clement* close to some well-known persecution by civil authorities. The two most obvious choices are the persecution by the emperor Nero in the midsixties or the persecution by the emperor Domitian in the midnineties. In either case, we might still hold Clement to have been the author, though the extent of his influence would have varied greatly according to his age during this forty-year span. If the Neronian date may be accepted, then *1 Clement* would be one of our oldest writings in the Apostolic Fathers. Most scholars have preferred the time of Domitian, however, with the recognition that there are arguments for either date.

With respect to the text of *1 Clement* itself, we find here the well-reasoned advice of a settled Christian community that sought to be of value in the disputed affairs of another church. The author (or authors) of the letter made a variety of appeals to the value of solid leadership within the faith community, as well as for the need to recognize a certain chain of apostolic authority in order to maintain a consistent ancestry of faith. There is an appeal to the figure of Moses in this effort, someone who had been chosen by God to lead the children of Israel through the wilderness and into the promised land of Canaan. As our author implies, it is inappropriate for any lineage of authority that God has ordained to lead the body of Christ to be removed by the whims and vagaries of human presumption. The text of *1 Clement* makes a general appeal to the need for obedience, faith, piety, and hospitality within the church. There is a call for humility and peace, as well as for the pursuit of a virtuous lifestyle. But most of all, there is a cry for love and repentance within the Corinthian church in the hope that, as the faith community would come to recognize the need for holiness in its midst, its membership would turn to respect divine authority and to set all things right and in order.

3. Didache

The word *Didache*, which is a Greek term for "teaching" or "instruction," has been used by ancient authors and modern commentators alike as an abbreviated reference to a work whose longer title is *The Teaching of the Lord to the Nations by the Twelve Apostles*. This composition is unique both with respect to its position in the collected writings of the Apostolic Fathers and its role within early Christian literature in general. Its sixteen brief chapters contain a variety of teaching materials that seem to have been used by a singular faith community around the end of the first century.

The text of the *Didache* may possibly have evolved through the process of several literary stages, including the collection of sources, the addition of original materials, and some secondary editorial work. The author of the *Didache* remains unknown, but often is referred to in academic circles simply as the "Didachist." It is unknown whether this person (or group) is also responsible for later editing that has occurred throughout the document.

As with the text of *Barnabas*, both the place and date of origin for the *Didache* remain uncertain. Possible geographic locations have been suggested along the eastern edge of the Mediterranean basin from Egypt to Asia Minor. But the most popular choice appears to be western Syria, and especially the ancient city of Antioch. With respect to the date of writing, some commentators in the early twentieth century placed the work as late as the fourth century. More recent researchers have argued that the sources behind the text, if not the text itself, may stem from as early as the middle of the first century. Most historians have argued for a late first-century origin, with some agreement that the final version of the work may not have been completed before the early second century.

The structure of the *Didache* may be easily divided into several major sections. The opening materials (chapters 1–6) are based upon the same "two ways" tradition that is reflected in a slightly modified form in *Barnabas* 18–21. Thereafter, the remaining passages may be roughly broken into three divisions: instructions for correct liturgical practices (chapters 7–11), instructions for community relationships (chapters 12–15), and a concluding set of admonitions about the coming of the end times (chapter 16). The basic theology of the text is primarily Jewish in tone. The sayings that are contained in the "two ways" materials are oriented toward an ethical lifestyle, focusing on the need to guard against temptations to break God's commandments. The liturgical and ecclesiastical

13

materials that follow contain a variety of traditions that stand parallel to other New Testament traditions, but are not based upon them. Thus, the *Didache* contains prayers that should be said at the community's "thanksgiving" meal (Eucharist?) in a style that is typically Jewish in form. Baptism is preferred in "living" (or moving) water, and visitors who come to the community in the name of the Lord are to be accepted without testing. All members of the community are counseled to be productive contributors to the life and faith of the church, to respect their leaders, and to live a lifestyle that is appropriate as followers of the commandments of God. The responsibilities of being a community of faith are a key to the Didachist's vision.

Modern scholars often consider the *Didache* to have been an ancient manual of instruction for early catechumens in the church. This is reinforced to some extent by the fact that later patristic authors made use of its materials both for the instruction of Christians in general and of the clergy specifically. It does not seem, however, that the various recommendations and rituals that the Didachist endorsed were widely followed throughout the Mediterranean church. Indeed, the limited usage of the materials that are preserved in this writing may have led to its eventual exclusion from mainstream Christianity. For this reason, we are truly fortunate to have at least one complete manuscript of the entire work available for research,[2] a Greek text that was only rediscovered and published in the late nineteenth century.

4. Epistles of Ignatius

One of the most important literary components of the Apostolic Fathers is a small collection of letters from the hand of Ignatius, an early bishop of Antioch in Syria. Ignatius was arrested by Roman authorities early in the second century, presumably because of his high profile as a leader of local Christians, and was taken under guard to his eventual martyrdom in Rome. The details of his arrest, his travel, and his execution remain unknown.[3] But we are fortunate to have some seven letters that he wrote to churches while in Asia Minor as he made his way toward his ultimate fate. These letters include correspondence with the communities of

Ephesus, Magnesia, Tralles, Rome, Philadelphia, Smyrna, and with the bishop Polycarp of Smyrna.[4] Their content provides a variety of insights into the theology of Ignatius and into the faith concerns that were at work in the church of the early second century. Furthermore, they afford us with additional information concerning some of the same Christian communities that Paul had visited a generation before.

Scholars recognize the existence of several basic issues that weighed heavily upon Ignatius and presumably the churches to which he wrote at the turn of the century. In the first instance, and perhaps foremost, Ignatius was greatly concerned for the existence of false doctrines and teachings that were being spread among the diverse Christian communities. This same apprehension over false teachings and misleading teachers is paralleled in New Testament writings from the late first century as well, including 1–3 John, the Gospels of Matthew and Luke, and Revelation. There seem to have been two primary courses along which these false teachings circulated. The first was a concerted effort by some within the church to return Christianity to its Jewish roots. The apostle Paul had already argued against this trend in his letter to Galatia, and Ignatius was even more adamant in his rejection of the idea. The second movement was directed toward a denial of the humanity of Jesus Christ, with a focus upon his divine nature. This idea, which was eventually labeled by the title "Docetism" and was condemned as a heresy by theologians in the later church, apparently held great appeal for those Christians who wished to sacrifice the human nature of the Messiah in favor of his divinity. Again, Ignatius found this particular brand of theology to be a genuine threat to the role that the Messiah played in the divine plan for human salvation—a true man dying for all humanity.

A second concern that Ignatius held was directed toward the appropriate form of clerical structure that was to be found among the churches. As bishop of Antioch, Ignatius believed that the church should only be directed by means of a threefold hierarchy of ecclesiastical offices: a single bishop, presbyters, and deacons. Within this configuration he envisioned that the bishop stood in the place of God, providing the ultimate direction of each faith community, that the presbyters acted in the role of God's divine counsel, and that the deacons served as a reflection of Jesus Christ.

While the church came to adopt this structure as a general form of administration for its numerous dioceses throughout the world, it is not clear that the design was so widely observed before the time of Ignatius. Indeed, Christianity may owe a great debt to the bishop for his insistence that this particular ecclesiastical system should serve as the basis for church organization.

Otherwise, the letters of Ignatius preserve a variety of early Christian creeds that he endorsed and that perhaps reflected the confessional practices of numerous early churches. His call for harmony and unity among Christians finds a close contemporary parallel in the thought of the author of *1 Clement*. His struggle to bring the early church into its own special place within the Roman world, separate from its Jewish heritage, undoubtedly led to the long decades of resistance that the Roman government showed to early Christian efforts at evangelization prior to the acceptance of the church under the rule of the emperor Constantine (ca. 285–337). Ultimately, Ignatius greatly influenced the later church and its theology and helped to usher into existence the primary direction that Christianity was eventually to pursue.

5. Epistle of Polycarp

Our collected writings include yet another letter from an important figure within the early church, the bishop Polycarp. A somewhat younger contemporary of Ignatius, Polycarp became the bishop of the church in Smyrna, located in western Asia Minor, and served in that capacity until his martyrdom at the age of eighty-six in the middle of the second century. We know that he had contact with Ignatius, since one letter in the Ignatian correspondence was sent to him.

Polycarp's own epistle, which is now divided into fourteen chapters, is addressed to the church of Philippi in northern Greece. It seems that the Philippians had approached Polycarp in his capacity as a friend of Ignatius and a respected leader of the church in Asia Minor with two primary concerns. The first issue appears to have been related to some anxiety that had arisen among the Philippian Christians with respect to a particular presbyter named Valens, whose greed had led him to conduct certain shameful actions in his role as a leader of the church there. The second matter seems to have been a request by the Philippians that Polycarp forward along to them any copies of letters by Ignatius that he might have in his possession. This latter request is not addressed in Polycarp's letter until chapter 13 and has led to the suggestion that the writing as we now have it may actually be a combination of two letters from the bishop, currently linked together into a single framework. Early Christian editors often combined writings from the same author as a way to save space on precious writing materials, thus shaping the works into a single manuscript.[5] Whether our work was originally one letter or two, it appears that Polycarp addressed the concerns of the Philippians some brief time after the journey of Ignatius to Rome, somewhere during the period of 105–135 C.E.

The primary value of Polycarp's letter is the discourse on the theme of "righteousness" that he offers in response to the situation of Valens. Much like the teachings of Ignatius before him, Polycarp envisions righteousness as the most complete expression of Christian unity that exists throughout the church. As he states, the qualities of righteousness that are worthy of Christ include a desire to avoid both scandal and false teaching. Righteousness includes both an ethical and a theological component. In an ethical sense, the good Christian should follow the commandments of God's will, endeavoring to avoid injustice, greed, love of money, slander, false testimony, and retaliation in anger for perceived injustices. Indeed, one should live for the benefit of the whole faith community rather than simply for one's own sake. In a theological sense, Polycarp aptly reflects the previous concerns of Ignatius when he warns against the foibles of Docetism. He specifically states that anyone who does not confess that Jesus Christ has come in the flesh is under the tyranny of such a false doctrine. It is clear that he, like Ignatius and the author of 1–3 John before him, was faced with a growing theological threat that must have circulated widely throughout the church at the turn of the century.

Polycarp offers a unique glimpse into the situation of Christians in the early second century. He provides a vision of what it means to live as worthy citizens of God's kingdom, a relatively new image that helped to shape the growing Christian consciousness of living an existence that transcended the daily life of Greek and Roman society. He also identifies the unique nature of Jesus Christ as the "eternal priest," an unusual understanding of the role of Jesus of Nazareth, whose only other parallel in early Christian literature is found in the New Testament book of Hebrews.

6. Martyrdom of Polycarp

It is appropriate at this point to mention another work that is associated with the tradition of the bishop Polycarp, that is, the literary description of his death. The *Martyrdom of Polycarp* is the only "martyrdom" account that is preserved among the works of the Apostolic Fathers. The story is offered as a firsthand depiction of the bishop's demise in the middle of the second century, perhaps penned during the years 155–160, or possibly a decade later. As it now stands, the details of the event have been captured as the basis of a letter of twenty-two chapters that was sent by the church in Smyrna to the congregation of Philomelium in central Asia Minor. The person who witnessed the martyrdom refers to himself as Evarestus, presumably a member of the church at Smyrna. His account has come to us through two manuscript traditions, the first being credited to Socrates of Corinth, who wrote down the words of an unknown Gaius, transcribed from the papers of Polycarp's disciple Irenaeus. And the second is attributed to Pionius, who recorded the words of an unknown Isocrates, again based upon the witness of Gaius.

There are several aspects to this martyrology that add color to our appreciation of early Christian history and interpretation. From the outset there are a large number of parallels between the arrest, trial, and execution of Polycarp and those of Jesus of Nazareth as depicted in the New Testament Gospels. For example, both men entered into the city of their death on a donkey and ultimately prayed for the safety of their followers. Both were the hosts of a final meal and were betrayed by someone who was familiar to them. Furthermore, both men were interrogated by someone named Herod and thereafter by a Roman official who sentenced them to death. In each instance we also witness the role of the Jews who, encouraged by the devil, insist upon the hero's execution. Such parallel elements reflect the early church's concern that the death of Jesus be seen against the backdrop of Old Testament expectation and fulfillment, as well as the desire to portray the execution of Polycarp against the idealized vision of the crucifixion of Jesus.

The role of the Jews in this process is a clear indicator of the early church's hostile response to the synagogue, which had rejected the Christian mission by the end of the first century. We have seen this already in the argument and language of *Barnabas*. And now we find it as a major element in the depiction of one of the ancient church's greatest leaders. The social, cultural, and political struggles between Judaism and its rejected sibling, Christianity, are readily apparent in the imagery and plot of the *Martyrdom*.

The execution of Polycarp is particularly significant in early Christian literature because of the framework that it provided for later depictions of the deaths of faithful followers of Christ. The early church, as first witnessed in the imagery of Ignatius, was greatly influenced by the famous martyrdom sequence of *2 Maccabees*, a graphic account of the struggle and persecution of pious Jews during the time of the Greek rule of Palestine under Antiochus Epiphanes IV. These stories of the faithful ones of God, who resisted all manner of torture and death for the sake of their beliefs, offered a unique image of the devoted martyr that came to serve as an example of piety both for Jews and Christians alike. Later Christian authors found this same image played out in the death of Polycarp and came to use the model of the bishop's arrest, trial, and execution as a scaffold for their own depictions of other martyrs from around the Mediterranean world. The faithful devotion of Polycarp, framed as a sweet sacrifice of trust, couched in a prayer of praise to God, and marked as the occasion for a "martyr's birthday," came to define the ideal role of a bishop within the church's faith tradition.

7. Second Clement

Common tradition has given the title of *2 Clement* to a work that most likely is not by the same author that produced the text of

1 Clement. In many respects the two writings are very different. For one thing, *2 Clement* is not a letter at all but an early sermon. It may in fact be the oldest complete sermon that remains from ancient Christian literature. In addition, both the language and theology of this text differ from that of *1 Clement*. One finds a concern that the reader must come to identify with a high Christology that has not been so explicitly stated in previous writings within the Apostolic Fathers. This christological focus, framed by the urgency of the end times, is based upon a very specific reading of prophecies from Isaiah and teachings by the apostle Paul. This concern for the end of time is offered as an impetus for Christians to respond with a lifestyle of faithful service and obedience to God.

Because of the uncertain origins behind *2 Clement*, it is very difficult to know how to place the text within the development of the early church. Scholars often argue that its title derived from the likelihood that the text was preserved together with *1 Clement* by the church in Corinth. With time, readers naturally came to assume that the same hand had produced both writings within a Roman setting. And it is certainly possible that a lone individual may have written both texts, one in the form of a letter and the other in the form of a sermon. But it is more likely that *2 Clement* was penned by someone else, perhaps a leader within the Corinthian church, possibly in response to the call of *1 Clement* for the Corinthians to be more righteous in their actions and more obedient in their response to God. Much of the imagery that is used throughout the text seems to reflect an intimate knowledge of Greek culture and its cultic games. Some scholars have argued that the work is actually from Alexandria, since its theology would have been easily at home within that setting. Other researchers have agreed with a Roman context, though they point to a later period in history, often identifying the second-century bishop Soter (ca. 166–174) as the creator of the work. The question of authorship thus remains unresolved. So too, the questions of place and date also remain unanswered, with speculation ranging from Italy to Greece to Egypt during the periods of the late first century to the late second century. In the turmoil of this quagmire, scholars typically place the text sometime during the early second century, leaving the question of provenance and authorship unsettled.

The text of *2 Clement* is particularly intriguing with respect to the specific issues that it addresses within its twenty chapters. From the outset readers are warned to turn away from the worship of dead gods, perhaps to suggest that the original audience was composed primarily of non-Jews. Thereafter, the author issues a call for obedience to the one, true God (chapters 3–14), an obedience that must be illustrated by a life of good works. Such actions are considered to be signs of a holy and righteous existence, just as love of one's neighbor is considered to be a reflection of one's love of God. Much like the warnings within the "two ways" tradition that have been preserved for us in *Barnabas* and the *Didache*, the author of *2 Clement* cautions each reader to avoid desires for material possessions and actions that break God's commandments. Instead, Christians should live according to pure motivations and thus be rewarded by passage into God's eternal kingdom.

In the final portion of the sermon our author turns toward the promised consummation of the world at the end of time (chapters 15–20). The image of prayer is offered as a guidepost for those who wish to avoid the pangs of death. The text counsels its readers not to be deceived by unrighteous people who appear to revel in earthly riches but to await their own reward in the world to come. As with the letters of Ignatius and Polycarp, the author of *2 Clement* seems to be well aware of false teachers who offer a different understanding of salvation and warns against such perverted teachings of the gospel message.

8. Shepherd of Hermas

Far and away the longest tractate within the Apostolic Fathers, the *Shepherd* contains a collection of sayings, parables, and apocalyptic imagery that reflects the various speculations of the church in the late first and early second centuries. The work has traditionally been divided into three primary sections: the *Visions*, the *Mandates* (or *Commandments*), and the *Similitudes* (or *Parables*). More recent scholars have reapportioned the text into 114 chapters for the sake of convenience: chapters 1–25 (= *Visions* 1–5), chapters 26–49 (= *Mandates* 1–12), and chapters 50–114 (= *Similitudes* 1–10).

The author of the *Shepherd* remains unknown. According to the narrative of the text, the events of the literary plot are told from the perspective of an early Christian by the name of Hermas, who was a slave of the Roman noblewoman Rhoda. His impure thoughts and sinful ways are addressed by several characters throughout the work, including a personification of the church in the form of a woman, appearing in various stages of life, and a figure known as the Shepherd, who offers detailed advice to Hermas about the nature of God's kingdom and the role of faithful Christians as citizens of that divine realm.

Scholars remain uncertain with respect to the origins of the *Shepherd*. It is entirely possible that the materials preserved here represent the collection of several different sets of teachings that have been brought together by an editor or group of editors in the second century. The age of these materials remains uncertain, however. There does not seem to be any dependence upon the teachings of Jesus, and New Testament foundations are not prominent, which might suggest that our sources are quite old within the literary history of the church. At the same time, however, our author's concern for apocalyptic images of the end time, the question of how many times a person's sins may be forgiven after baptism (or penance), the nature of the Holy Spirit, and the process by which the church is constructed all suggest that some long period of theological speculation has already occurred by the time of writing. Most scholars agree that the text should be assigned to the church in Italy, most likely to Rome specifically. But the composition of the work, or at least its final compilation, can only be broadly dated to sometime within the second century.

The book of the *Shepherd* contains a number of interesting images, though the length and repetition of those images eventually lead to a lack of interest among most readers long before reaching the end of the work. As with *1 Clement* above, the context of the *Shepherd* suggests a period of struggle for the church. There is no distinction made between the roles of bishop and presbyter throughout the text, nor does our author appeal to such ecclesiastical offices as the authority for the teachings offered here. Specific teachings and parables from the church's tradition make up a bulk of the writing. The reader is expected to read these materials through the lens of allegory, thereby coming to recognize the importance of the Holy Spirit in the activities of the world and in the construction of the church. A significant portion of the *Shepherd* is devoted to the value of virtues in the life of the Christian, as well as the need to respect the purity of interpersonal relationships.

The *Shepherd* offers an insightful glimpse into the ways in which the early church came to gather the remembrance of their experiences of religious wisdom into narrative collections of teaching. The core of these materials reflects the insights of faith communities, churches that grew in their appreciation of what it meant to reside in a life of faith within an increasingly hostile society. As a result, our editor has produced a unique writing that was widely recognized and employed by later Christian authors as the foundation of ethical instruction and a radical vision of the evolving church.

9. Epistle to Diognetus

There is only one text among the Apostolic Fathers that may be classified under the heading of an "apology" or defense for the Christian faith, and that is the *Epistle to Diognetus*. A brief work of only twelve chapters, *Diognetus* illustrates the typical concerns of Christian authors in the late second and early third centuries, including such writers as Justin Martyr, Melito of Sardis, and Athenagoras of Athens. Most important here is the author's desire to provide a firm rationale for the existence of the church in the midst of Jewish and pagan claims for religious priority.

Unfortunately, we know little about the background of the epistle. The opening line of the work indicates that the text was addressed to someone named Diognetus, which some scholars believe to have been the Alexandrian procurator Claudius Diogenes, who ruled at the end of the second century. But this remains uncertain. Other scholars have argued that our text is actually the lost *Apology of Quadratus* that was addressed to the emperor Hadrian early in the second century, a letter whose existence we know from Eusebius of Caesarea.[6] But again, this suggestion is based upon speculation only. The only known copy of the work (which sadly was destroyed in the Franco-Prussian War of 1870) had been collected together with various writings from

23

Justin Martyr, a fact that has led some researchers to favor Justin as the author. Most scholars reject this option, preferring other possibilities, such as Melito of Sardis, Hippolytus of Rome, Theophilus of Antioch, and Pantaenus of Alexandria. In reality, both our author and the date of the writing remain uncertain. The text typically is dated to the latter half of the second century and attributed to an unknown Christian writer.

The content of *Diognetus* actually appears to be the compilation of two different works. The epistle itself, which seeks to defend the validity of the Christian faith in the midst of religious competitors, seems to extend from the beginning of the text through chapter 10. The remaining materials (chapters 11–12) appear to be more of a homily directed toward the theme of the "Word of God." The transition from one section to the next was marked in our manuscript tradition by an empty space, perhaps suggesting the end of one work and the beginning of another. Otherwise, both the theme and literary style of the writing change dramatically as *Diognetus* comes to a close in its final two chapters.

Like the other apologies that are known from early Christian literature, *Diognetus* follows the typical concerns of a well-educated author who is attempting to convince a specific audience of the value of Christianity as a faith. It is possible that our letter was addressed to a particular reader by the name of Diognetus. But it is just as likely that our author intended the work for anyone who might question the right of the church to stand as a witness of assurance to the glory of God.

The opening chapters of *Diognetus* are addressed to the follies of both Jewish and pagan religious and liturgical practices. For our author, pagans partake in the worship of dead idols that have been created by humans, while Jews participate in useless customs and rituals. Christians are uniquely distinct, however, because they live in the world as the soul resides in the body. They are rejected for their beliefs and actions, but remain true to the service of God and society through their lifestyles. In the final chapters our author turns to the figure of Christ as the living witness of God's concern for humanity. As Christ has been sent for deliverance from sin and death, so too God has planted a garden of love in which all believers may come to share in the fruit of salvation. In only a few well-constructed chapters our author has addressed the basic issues of the typical early Christian apology: the folly of false religions, the preeminence of Christianity, the need for repentance, and the hope of human salvation through Christ and the love of God.

10. Fragments of Papias

The final group of writings that is typically included among the writings of the Apostolic Fathers does not offer a single text at all, but a collection of fragmentary materials that are associated with the name of Papias. A contemporary of Polycarp, Papias was the bishop of Hierapolis in Asia Minor and was best known for his text *Expositions of the Sayings of the Lord*. This five-volume work has unfortunately been lost to history, but some few fragments from its contents have been preserved in various early Christian writings, including the ancient church history of Eusebius of Caesarea.

The fragments included in our collection represent two strains of tradition that are associated with the name of Papias: sources that are from his pen and (presumably) stem from his *Expositions* and materials about his life within the post-apostolic tradition. Scholars are divided with respect to the extent of materials that should be included here. Certain traditions clearly reflect the tradition of Papias, while others (particularly from more recent authors) may offer only the slightest value to modern research.

Undoubtedly the most important materials from the witness of Papias relate to reminiscences concerning the development of New Testament literature. It was Papias, for example, who preserved the tradition that Mark made note of the recollections of the apostle Peter as a written testimony to the words and deeds of the Lord. And it was also Papias who documented that Matthew recorded the sayings of Jesus in Hebrew in order that each person could translate them into their own language and context. In addition, the witness of Papias provides a unique link between apostolic tradition and the post-apostolic church, since, as Eusebius argues, Papias had heard John (the apostle?) and was a companion of Polycarp. Such fragmentary traditions and testimony to ancient links between scattered Christians have gone a long way toward the development of historical assumptions about the evolution of our New Testament canon and the apostolic witness that it reflects.

But the sources that Papias has offered also provide intriguing glimpses into early Christian speculation about events that lie beyond the scope of scripture. Thus, for example, we hear that Judas Iscariot wandered the earth for some great period of time before his death, bloated beyond recognition and suffering innumerable torments of flesh and spirit. And it seems that Papias was highly dependent upon the teachings of Aristion, a "disciple of the Lord" who remains unnamed in the New Testament and from whom Papias appears to have derived much of his information. Indeed, Aristion is typically linked with the names of the twelve apostles as the caretaker of ancient authoritative traditions. There is little question that the recollections of Papias have provided ample contributions to the development of second-century views of the apostles and the foundation of the great church tradition. The inclusion of his testimony makes a fitting, if illusive, conclusion to most modern editions of the Apostolic Fathers.

CHAPTER 2

People and Places

N ow that we have introduced the texts that form the collected works of the Apostolic Fathers, it is important to gain
some general awareness of the spread of Christianity
through the end of the second century. Our knowledge of the
extended reach of the church during this period varies according
to literary and archeological remains. Much information is available about those Christians who lived in highly populated areas,
particularly in the foremost cities of the Roman Empire, while few
details remain about more isolated and rural communities that
sprang up around the Mediterranean. Most importantly, we must
be careful not to let our modern prejudices about the popular traditions of Christian history guide our assumptions about the character of people and places that actually remain something of a
mystery to us.

From the outset it is crucial to remember that our principal
knowledge of the first generation of Christians has been highly
shaped by materials both by and about the apostle Paul that were
preserved for us in the New Testament. His speculation about the
significance of the cross and resurrection of Christ Jesus has had a
paramount effect upon subsequent Christian theology. Indeed,
what he offered through his correspondence with scattered
churches around the Mediterranean world, together with the later

witness of the book of Acts, often deceives us into the conviction that he was the first Christian to evangelize the world outside of Palestine. In fact, nothing could be further from the truth. We find, for example, that in Acts he was sent to arrest Christians who already were active in Damascus[1] and that he encountered Christian communities in Asia Minor and Greece during his travels throughout those regions.[2] Most scholars agree that Paul was the beneficiary of many faithful supporters along his journeys. His letters contain a range of hymns, ethical teachings, liturgical materials, and prayers that he certainly accumulated as he undertook his missionary endeavors, taking what were often local traditions from one church to the next and subsequently making them universal practices.

At the same time it seems quite likely that Paul's theological perspective was shaped and informed by early Christian thinkers who lived in the communities that he visited. The author of Acts has already indicated that the apostle first received instruction from Ananias in Damascus, which Paul himself seems to suggest took a period of three years.[3] Otherwise, we find that some of his foundational assumptions about Christianity appear to have matured and taken solid form during his ministry, including a transition from his initial focus upon the imminent return of Christ toward a more pastorally sensitive consideration of the roles of ecclesiastical leadership. Ultimately, as both Ignatius and Polycarp recognized, Paul was clearly a dominant contributor to the life and thought of early Christianity. But he was certainly not the first and only donor.

Another element of early church history must be recognized within the nature of faith communities themselves. With respect to early Christianity, scholars often speak of "the church" in such and such a city or region. For most students this gives the false impression that each particular town or city supported an individual faith community that worshiped together and maintained a common fellowship of teachings and theological principles. While such situations may indeed have existed in very small towns or rural areas, the mainstream activities of early Christians were quite the opposite.

We must not forget that the earliest Christians were Jewish in background and found support for their beliefs among certain members of the local synagogue. As the author of Acts informs us, Paul himself often visited synagogues throughout his missionary journeys, both to worship with fellow Jews and to seek out others like himself who shared similar Christian inclinations. Many of these Christian Jews eventually agreed to meet together apart from the traditional setting of the synagogue, but they rarely abandoned that common location altogether. Indeed, the synagogue was not just a place for worship, but served as the cultural center, bank, and internal forum for Jewish community activities throughout the Mediterranean world. Large cities typically served as a home for numerous synagogues. By the same token, those same cities came to host numerous "house churches," the individual homes of Christians in which believers could say their special prayers, sing their favorite hymns, observe their unique liturgical practices, and spread the teachings of their faith among themselves and their children.

Thus, when we say "the church" in such and such a city, we typically mean the combined house churches that existed there. In the first century many of these communities operated with only a minimum of significant interaction. Their faith was individualistic and undoubtedly evolved through the local customs of a particular group, having more the feel of a cult than of an organized religion. By the second century, however, a structure of general oversight had begun to develop by which certain leaders within the larger community had come to function as administrators (presbyters and bishops) for churches within a given area. Such associations became the foundational model for the modern configuration of dioceses existing throughout much of the church today. Of course, at the start of the second century this arrangement was not firmly established among the broader churches of the Mediterranean basin. And without such a centralized structure one might expect to find various faith groups that were quite dissimilar in their recognition of an appropriate Christian lifestyle and in their acceptance of a suitable expression of theology for those who wanted to worship Jesus of Nazareth as the Christ. It is little wonder then that the authors of the Apostolic Fathers spent so much of their time and energy during this same period in an effort to establish the parameters of Christian ethics and theology. Their church was exceedingly complex. Their audiences were exceptionally diverse.

1. Italy

The amount of information that is available about the spread of the church in Italy outside of Rome through the late second century is not extensive. As with the rest of the Mediterranean world, there appears to have been primarily a scattering of smaller faith communities. Some of these practiced a form of proto-orthodoxy that eventually became accepted into the broad "catholic" church of the empire. Some observed the popular beliefs of Gnosticism that were taught and practiced by a variety of worshipers. By the middle of the second century some were practitioners of Marcion's teachings (Marcionites) and, by the last half of that century, others observed the cultic instruction of Montanus (the founder of Montanism, the so-called Phrygian heresy). Not all of these groups would today be classified as "Christian" by the rigid standards of orthodoxy that the church uses to define itself in the modern world. But in the apostolic and post-apostolic periods, the devotees of these various forms of messianic worship undoubtedly all considered themselves to be followers of "the Way" in some respect.

We are aware of various centers of Christianity and their remains throughout Italy. Specifically, there was a renowned church at Syracuse in Sicily, though debate persists as to whether the origins of that community existed long before the third century. Farther up the road on the Italian peninsula we know of churches at Puteoli, Cumae, Campania, Antium, and Ostia. The author of Acts states that Paul was received by Christians when he arrived in Puteoli,[4] and the *Acts of Peter* indicates that Peter and his companion Theon found the same Christians there some time later.[5] Cumae is the site to which Hermas, the narrator of the *Shepherd*, states that he was traveling when he first had his visions. This seems appropriate, since the area was renowned as the home of Sibylline prophecy and visions. Campania had a large Jewish community that in part turned toward Christianity in the second century. Antium, the home of the emperor Nero, was a refuge to which Pope Victor sent the deacon Callistus (ca. 190) with the support of a small allowance and the care of local Christians. And Ostia, the port of ancient Rome, was the reputed site of the great debate between the Christian Octavius and the pagan Caecilius in the late second century, according to the *Octavius* of Minicius Felix. Sadly, no church buildings survive there from before the fourth century. All of these locations offer some hint of the early church in Italy. But of course, the dominant city of interest was and remains the capital of the empire, Rome.

The church of Rome is featured at several points in the literature of the New Testament and Apostolic Fathers. With respect to the New Testament, we recall Paul's letter to the Romans as the finest statement of his theological beliefs, ideas that were sent to a Christian community that he had never visited. The book of Acts recalls Paul's eventual journey to the city while under arrest, a trip that stands as the climax of the textual narrative.

Yet some question remains about the extent to which we may know the Roman church through these scriptural witnesses. For example, the author of Acts seems far more concerned with Paul's journey to Rome than with his time spent among Christians while there. Indeed, Acts concludes with only brief comments that Paul lived by himself in Rome for two years at his own expense, meeting with the leaders of the Jews in an effort to convince them of the validity of his faith in the Lord Jesus Christ. Rome's Christians are never actually mentioned. This may seem to be especially surprising in the light of Paul's letter, a text that is delivered with confidence and conviction. But we recall that Paul addressed the Roman church on the basis of reputation and not through personal knowledge. The concluding chapter of Romans, replete with greetings to various individuals within the church, may be an attempt to make connections in a situation where Paul had no other personal association with the local leadership.

At the same time, however, we learn something of great importance from Paul's letter to Rome, that is, that the church there was divided between Jewish Christians and those of non-Jewish background. This seems patently clear from the nature of Paul's shifting argument, which is sometimes addressed with respect for Jewish traditions and at other times in support of believers who do not share in the heritage of Israel. The apostle undoubtedly recognized the tension that a diverse background of experiences brought to efforts at Christian unity. Nonetheless, such a tension would have been tolerable to the extent that believers were divided among scattered house churches throughout the city.

31

The Apostolic Fathers shed some additional light upon the situation. The letter of Ignatius to Rome, written in a style that is reminiscent of Paul, continues to praise the reputation of the Roman church without naming any particular leader. It is true that Ignatius, like Paul, had no personal experience with the church there. But it is quite odd that he makes no specific appeal to a bishop or group of presbyters by the time of his writing in the early second century. Of course, the text of *1 Clement*, which was penned by the Roman church at some point prior to the witness of Ignatius, likewise does not name either its author or the ecclesiastical authority by which it feels justified to address the concerns of the church at Corinth. This has led some scholars to argue that, despite claims for Roman apostolic succession by the historian Eusebius of Caesarea, the ecclesiastical hierarchy of the city was not firmly solidified until after the first century. Indeed, the scattered presence of Rome's Christians and the diversity of theological views that existed within the city would explain how a single church could produce such sundry texts as *1 Clement* and the *Shepherd of Hermas*, writings that appear to reflect almost contradictory views of church structure and authority. And this is not to mention other texts that often are attributed to Rome as well, writings such as *2 Clement* and the New Testament texts of 1–2 Peter and Hebrews.

Two names are often mentioned with respect to the leadership of the church in Rome that must be considered here: Clement of Rome and bishop Soter. Of the numerous persons who we know to have been a part of that faith community, only these are viewed as possible authors of texts that are now preserved in the Apostolic Fathers.

With reference to Soter, little is known. Perhaps originally from Campania, he appears to have served as bishop during the reign of Marcus Aurelius (161–180). Scholars note that Easter was first celebrated as an annual feast in Rome during his tenure. He supported the work of the church in Corinth, as is indicated by the response of Dionysius of Corinth to Soter's letter to the Corinthian church, and may have been the author of *2 Clement*, according to some scholars.

Clement, on the other hand, has been the focus of several interpretive traditions. Believed by some early Christians to have been ordained by the apostle Peter himself,[6] he is usually argued to be Rome's third bishop (ca. 88–ca. 97) after Linus and Anacletus. This assumes, of course, that the role of bishop was firmly established in Rome many years before the end of the first century. The author of the *Shepherd* mentions him as someone worthy to be given a copy of the teachings that Hermas received, thereafter to share them with churches in cities abroad.[7] Though no specific ecclesiastical title is assigned to Clement in the *Shepherd*, we may safely assume that he was a person of importance within the Roman church.

According to the later Clementine *Homilies* and *Recognitions*, Clement's pedigree should be associated with the heritage of a noble Roman citizenship, related by birth to the family of the Caesars. While exceedingly difficult to confirm, such connections would explain how the church in Rome was able to survive the turmoil of civil and religious struggle that was typical of Roman society and culture until the reign of Constantine the Great. Clement's influence upon the growth and organization of Roman Christianity toward the end of the first century remains primarily speculative, of course. Yet his reputation as a qualified and reputable leader nonetheless endures.

2. Greece

The situation of Christianity in Greece during the first two centuries is much better documented than it is for Italy. The book of Acts mentions several sites where Paul either encountered Christians or established missions during his journeys. These include settings like Philippi, Thessalonica, Beroea, Athens, and Corinth. And with respect to several of these communities, we have letters from the hand of the apostle himself that detail the problems and concerns that individual churches faced as they came to understand what it meant to be the body of Christ. Otherwise, a number of additional locations are known to have arisen by the late second century, including churches at Apollonia (of Thrace), Larissa, Aegina, Cenchreae, Lacedaemon, Patras, Same, and Nicopolis. For the most part these sites were considered to endorse orthodox theology and acceptable liturgical practices as defined by later ecclesiastical standards. Unlike Italy, the church in Greece appears to have been less influenced by heterodoxy in its structural evolution, though it certainly endured many struggles in the process.

The two primary centers of Greek Christianity that are reflected in the Apostolic Fathers are Philippi and Corinth. The Philippians' queries to Polycarp served as the occasion of his letter to them. In a similar manner, it was the Corinthians who had contacted the church at Rome, thereby precipitating the circumstances under which the text of *1 Clement* was penned. And, of course, the sermon that is preserved in *2 Clement* may either have been addressed to Corinth from some foreign location or, perhaps, may have been preached and recorded within the Corinthian church itself. These two cities will be our present focus, but we must first survey the remaining centers of Greek Christianity as background to what follows.

Moving from east to west as one crosses the Greek peninsula, we encounter three early Christian communities in southern Macedonia.[8] The town of Apollonia on the Aegean Sea was established at the beginning of the fifth century B.C.E., flourished under the reign of Philip of Macedon, and gained importance from its proximity along the Egnatian Way. Though little is known about the church in this city, its location midway between Aphipolis in Macedonia and Thessalonica would have made the site a natural location for Christianity to gain a foothold. The church at Thessalonica is somewhat better known. The author of Acts suggests that Paul and Silas actually established the faith community that arose in the city. And Paul's own letters there are among his earliest on record. Home to a variety of religious cults, the city was a favorite vacation spot because of its renowned hot springs, a factor that made it an issue of debate between Roman Catholic and Greek Orthodox bishops as they continually reapportioned their spheres of influence over the centuries. The last known church of the region was in Beroea, another site where Paul and Silas may have established Christianity's roots. By tradition, Philemon's slave Onesimus came to serve as the first bishop there.

Several churches are recognized from the southern areas of Greece, though their origins are not entirely clear. On the eastern coast, Christianity took root in Larissa, a city whose intellectual climate spawned the likes of Hippocrates and Pindar. Further south, the city of Athens hosted a Pauline visit, though the author of Acts offers no suggestion that the apostle founded the church there. Indeed, we do not hear much else of Athenian Christianity until the second century when Melito of Sardis noted that the emperor Hadrian (117–138) had written against persecution of Christians in Thessalonica, Larissa, and Athens.[9] The church in Athens was apparently slow in its growth and incorporated the influence of numerous outsiders among its leadership, including the early bishops Narkissos of Palestine and Publius of Malta. Publius was martyred in the latter half of the second century. The Athenian bishop Quadratus is credited for an early Christian apology, a fragment of which is now sometimes associated with the *Epistle to Diognetus*. The Athenian Aristides is also known to have written an apology to the emperor Marcus Aurelius. Other churches in southern Greece from the first and second centuries include communities on the island of Aegina, Cenchreae, and Lacedaemon (Sparta). There is little to be known about the Christians at these locations, except that Paul mentions Phoebe as a deaconess of the church at Cenchreae.[10] This indicates that Christianity had been established quite early in the area, though it is impossible to know whether the church there should be linked with Paul's visit to the region as he traveled from Corinth to Ephesus.

Christianity on the western coast of Greece may be traced to locations such as Patras, Same, and Nicopolis. We know little of early Christians in these cities, except that the New Testament mentions Nicopolis as a location where Paul hoped to winter as he awaited the arrival of Titus.[11] The region was heavily influenced by the power structures of Corinth and typically attracted the attention of Roman authorities because of its relatively close proximity to the Italian coastline.

This brings us to the city of Corinth, which served to govern the affairs of numerous local towns and communities. The Corinthian church is seemingly well known from Paul's letters in the New Testament and the text of *1 Clement* in the Apostolic Fathers. It was a community that found itself in close confrontation with a variety of foreign cultures and religious traditions. But in many respects, it was undoubtedly much like many ancient seaports of the period.

What appears to be most evident about the Corinthian situation is the tension within the community with respect to traditions and authority. With reference to tradition, Paul soon found himself in a continuing dialogue with the local church concerning Eucharistic practices, ethical issues, and questions of legitimacy. This struggle is explained to some extent by the observation that his teachings were offered in competition with those of other early evangelists, namely, Apollos and Cephas (Peter). But at the same time there can be little question that the Corinthians were unfamiliar with an understanding of Christianity that was essentially linked to strict Jewish guidelines. Or, at least, the various house churches within the city were not in agreement with respect to their dependence upon Judaism's religious customs and culture.

With reference to authority, we not only discover that Paul was forced to repeat his assertion that he had divine approval for his right to leadership but also that such issues continued to resurface long after the apostle left. This is made evident in *1 Clement*. As with the situation of Athens mentioned above, it seems that the Corinthians were often forced to turn to outsiders when confronted with issues of leadership and guidance. In any case, the fact that Paul spent almost two years in the area suggests that Christianity was quite active by the middle of the first century. His correspondence with the church indicates that numerous Christians visited the city from other locations during the course of their travels.

Finally, we return to the beginning of our survey to mention the Macedonian church of Philippi. Repatriated as a Roman colony by Mark Antony in the late first century B.C.E., the city was governed by "Italian law" as a center of imperial authority. According to the author of Acts, the church in Philippi seems to have been established by Paul and Silas, and its struggles with the local Jewish population were considerable. Presumably the Philippian church continued to grow and gain prominence as is evidenced by its contact in the second century with Polycarp. Archeological remains indicate the presence of a large church structure that was in use from that same time period. As Paul states toward the end of his letter to the city,[12] the Christians of Philippi were able to provide him with much needed resources, suggesting that there were considerable financial assets available for use by the local community. It is most reasonable that many of these believers had financial means by which to support their religious convictions.

3. Asia Minor

It is impossible to review in such a limited space all of the known church communities and theological variations that existed in Asia Minor during the first two centuries of Christian expansion. The author of Acts alone mentions that Paul and his companions worked in the towns and cities of Tarsus, Seleucia, Derbe, Lystra, Pisidian Antioch, Iconium, Troas, Ephesus, and Miletus. The author of Revelation likewise notes the presence of other churches in Smyrna, Pergamum, Thyatira, Sardis, Philadelphia, and Laodicea. And among the Apostolic Fathers, Ignatius addresses additional Christian communities that were located in Magnesia and Tralles, while the author(s) of the *Martyrdom of Polycarp* wrote to the church in Philomelium. So too, we should certainly include churches at Colossae, Apamea, Eumeneia, Otrus, Tymion, Pepuza, Nicomedia, Amastris, Sinope, Amisus, Melitene, and Laranda. Many of these locations reveal some evidence of Christian activity during the first and second centuries, but specific knowledge of the growth of the church and its actions are often quite limited. At the same time, however, there were a large number of churches in Asia Minor that had a tremendous impact upon the rise of ancient Christianity, as well as a specific and immediate influence upon certain authors among the Apostolic Fathers.

There was a distinct tendency among Christian leaders in Asia Minor to speculate about the nature of theology. Indeed, it was this attitude toward creative conjecture that led to the very controversies behind the writings of Ignatius as he traveled toward his ultimate martyrdom in Rome. Common tradition has long pointed an incriminating finger at the church in Ephesus, for example, as the home of innovative theological perceptions that came to form the backbone of the theology that permeates the Gospel of John. And the author of Revelation offered the resiliency of loose ideas among churches in Asia Minor as a backdrop to the long apocalyptic discourse that dominates the bulk of that text. For the moment, it will be important for us to examine such ideas at work within the region, focusing specifically upon the communities that Ignatius addresses along his journey, with a primary nod to the city of Smyrna, home of the bishop Polycarp.

Among the better-known churches to which Ignatius writes was the faith community in Ephesus. Paul himself had spent some considerable time in the region, having found that a circle of believers was already present when he arrived. According to Acts 18–19, there was some confusion within the local church about the teachings of Apollos, the nature of true baptism, and the role of the Holy Spirit in the life of the believer. The New Testament letter to Ephesus that is attributed to Paul suggests that the community was in need of instruction about how to live an appropriate Christian lifestyle as the body of Christ, as well as the proper approach by which to structure the church according to a suitable hierarchical order. It is most interesting that popular religious tradition has associated the Gospel of John and the Johannine epistles within this same community, since that particular Gospel reveals no particular concern for the authoritative role of an "apostle" or for a framework by which to govern the church. Instead, the voice of Jesus in the Gospel of John seems to indicate that all believers are directly responsible to the Son of God in the same way that the Son is responsible to the Father. Theologically, the universal church found such an idea to be persuasive; ecclesiastically, however, Christians were not satisfied with such a loose system of governance.

Thus we find Ignatius in conversation with the Ephesians with respect to his two primary concerns: leadership hierarchy and correct doctrine. On the first count, Ignatius acknowledges the presence of a bishop within the community (Onesimus), yet offers a concerted focus upon the need for harmony among the faithful and an acceptance of three offices (bishop-presbyter-deacon) as necessary for suitable governance. The presence of this theme among the writings of Ignatius has convinced many scholars that his teachings reflected the common practice of the time. In fact, however, while we find Ignatius speaking with boldness about his own preferences for church order and structure, these ideas may have been only gradually coming into acceptance around the Mediterranean world. And so the situation in Ephesus could have been much more fluid than many modern Christians realize. On the second count, correct doctrine, Ignatius preaches against the influence both of those who wished to return Christianity to its Jewish roots (Judaizers) and of those who wished to deny the humanity of Jesus (Docetists). The first problem was already addressed by Paul, and apparently was a typical foil for many early Christian preachers until the final split between the church and synagogue around the beginning of the second century. The second problem was also common among ancient theologians, especially in the eastern Mediterranean, as is witnessed in 1–3 John and Revelation. The great ecumenical church councils eventually resolved the issue theologically in later centuries.

Two other churches to which Ignatius wrote, Magnesia on the Meander River and Tralles, are lesser known today. Like Ephesus, the city of Magnesia harbored the cult of Artemis, which was avidly revered by many local citizens. As Ignatius observes in his letter, a bishop, presbyters, and deacons already were in place in the local church by the time of his journey. He names some of these individuals for us: Damas (bishop), Bassus and Apollonius (presbyters), and Zotion (deacon). Otherwise, we do not know of any other bishops from the Magnesian church prior to Eusebius who attended the Council of Sardis in 343. With respect to Tralles, Ignatius once again acknowledges the presence of a thriving church community, naming a bishop (Polybius) and calling for respect to be shown to presbyters and deacons within the church. In his letters to Magnesia and Tralles he warns against those who were teaching the false doctrine of Docetism and calls for his readers to remain blameless and unified in their faith.

Two other cities deserve quick notice here. Ignatius writes to Philadelphia as a church of firmly established harmony under the strong leadership of a single bishop. The author of Revelation observed that the Philadelphian church was confronted with Jewish opposition, and Ignatius confirms this same tendency when he warns against those who are teaching Judaism within the community. Undoubtedly, the religious enthusiasm of Christians had led to many conversions among the Jews, thus to fan the wrath of the local synagogue. The most influential cult in the city was that of Dionysus, the god of vines and wine, which may explain why Ignatius also advised the local church to "stay away from evil plants not cultivated by Jesus Christ"[13] as a metaphorical warning to avoid competing cults.

Finally, we must certainly mention the city of Smyrna, whose church was addressed by Ignatius and whose bishop, Polycarp, wrote his own letter to Philippi and was the subject of adoration by the author(s) of the *Martyrdom of Polycarp*. Smyrna was in close competition with Ephesus as the chief city of Asia. The author of Revelation notes that the church at Smyrna, like Philadelphia, was in constant struggle with the local synagogue. The *Martyrdom* gives some additional evidence of this struggle in the late second century. The structure of the church seems to have fit the pattern of bishop, presbyters, and deacons. And the presence of Polycarp as a wise leader who lived to a great age brought the community great fame within later church history. Once again, Ignatius warns the Christians of Smyrna to avoid false teachers who deny that Christ came in the flesh. Indeed, he even argues that the elements of the Eucharist remain as the blood and flesh of the Savior, despite what some in the church there seemed to argue. Smyrna was a center of the imperial cult of Rome, having been chosen as a site for the first local temple in honor of the emperor Tiberius (built in 23 C.E.). In the *Martyrdom* we see the pride that this instilled in local citizens, which is reflected in cries for the death of Polycarp as an "atheist."

4. Syria and Palestine

As with Asia Minor, there were a variety of early churches that existed throughout both Syria and Palestine during our period. Some of these locations are rather well known, large metropolitan areas such as Antioch and Edessa in Syria, and Jerusalem and Caesarea Maritima in Palestine. Early Christian literature and archeological finds suggest the presence of Christians at other lesser-known cities of the first and second centuries, including (north to south) Rhossus, Laodicea, Apamea, Tripolis, Damascus, Sidon, Tyre, Ptolemais, Sebaste, Joppa, and Azotus. But most of these secondary sites had little influence upon the development of texts that are now preserved in the Apostolic Fathers. Furthermore, what can be said about such churches from the evidence that is available probably does not add much to our general knowledge of Christianity in the region. Our primary focus will be upon the cities of Jerusalem and Antioch. In the case of Jerusalem, some of our earliest testimony concerning the rise of the church is related to the city, though the influence of Christians there quickly waned in the second half of the first century. With respect to Antioch, its Christians served as one of the primary launching platforms both for the missionary work of the apostle Paul and for the last journey of Ignatius to Rome.

As elsewhere throughout the Mediterranean world, Christianity in Syria-Palestine was deeply indebted to and dependent upon the spread of synagogues. Our knowledge of the church in the area indicates that Judaism had given it a distinct, religious framework. The influence of Judaism is most noticeable in the theological tension that arose when non-Jews sought to enter the ranks of the Christian mission there. This process was paralleled elsewhere in the Roman Empire, of course, especially in many cities of Asia Minor where the church first gained a firm foothold and rose with power to compete against traditional cultic faiths among local citizens. But in the region of Syria-Palestine, the roots of Judaism were clearly the most evident.

Let us begin with a review of Jerusalem. According to the witness of the author of Acts, it was in Jerusalem and its environs that the earliest church stumbled into existence. It is here that we read about the exploits of the apostles Peter and John and about the death of John's brother, James. It is here that we find the establishment of the office of deacon within the church, as well as the notation that the first deacons were expected to serve the needs of the "Hellenists" who had been attracted to the early Christian message. It is here that we discover the martyrdom of the deacon Stephen, the fledgling efforts of Paul and Barnabas to discover their own unique mission within the church, and the disaster that befell Ananias and Sapphira when they schemed to withhold their property from the church.

What is perhaps most telling about the situation of Christians in Jerusalem is the faith community's efforts to establish something of a socialist commune as the foundational structure for ecclesiastical polity. As the author of Acts observes, these earliest Christians held all things in common, sharing possessions, praying, and breaking bread together. Though no explanation for this communal effort is ever offered, one might speculate that the early theology of the Jerusalem church held that the return of Christ was imminent. Thus, there would be no use in any efforts to engage the typical problems of daily living and wage earning. In its most basic cultic stage, the church viewed its existence through a recognition that it served God in a brief, temporal age. But, of course, this attempt to define the parameters of a suitable Christian lifestyle ultimately proved to be seriously flawed. Thus, it sometimes seems that the apostle Paul is constantly collecting funds for the "poor of Jerusalem."

We must assume that the picture of the church in Jerusalem that Acts portrays is highly stylized to be an ideal expression of what later Christians remembered of the situation at the end of the first century. Archeological evidence is only of limited help in this effort, since one can never be certain whether artifacts from the first century are strictly Jewish or, instead, to be identified with messianic Judaism, that is, what we would now call Christianity. In either case, the author of Acts recalls that the early Jerusalem Christians were often persecuted and suggests that such struggles were inspired by the Holy Spirit while seeking to spread the Christian message around the Mediterranean. Ultimately, most of what we might know about the church in this region disappeared after the Jewish wars of 66–73, that time when the Temple was destroyed by Rome and both Jews and Christians fled the area as an act of self-preservation.

The situation of Christianity in Jerusalem and its environs holds little direct relevance for the Apostolic Fathers, since none of our texts has been attributed to that region. But the flight of numerous Jewish Christians from the city in the seventies is most significant because many of these faithful came to the city of Antioch in Syria. The book of Acts notes that Antioch was a central staging point for Paul's missionary work, a fact that Paul himself seems to acknowledge in his letter to the Galatians. What we know about the city is that it played host to different types of early Christian perspectives, including both the more conservative teachings of Peter and James and the more liberal views of Paul and (presumably) Barnabas. Already the home of a large Jewish population prior to the first century, it was only natural that Antioch was to spawn a wide variety of views within the realm of early Christian theology. Indeed, some of Christianity's most vibrant thinkers spent time in

42

Antioch and western Syria, including Paul and Barnabas, Ignatius and Tatian, the famous Gnostics Basilides and Cerdo, and the theologians Origen and Lucian.

But the key to understanding Antioch's contribution to early Christian origins is clearly the same as that which characterized the church in Rome. The church in Antioch was composed of a series of house churches that spawned from the individual legacies of synagogues that were scattered throughout the metropolis. Some of these house churches were undoubtedly somewhat open-minded with respect to the inclusion of non-Jews within the early Christian faith, while others were probably more careful about observing Jewish ethical guidelines and institutional rituals. Hence, early Christian literature suggests that the situation in Antioch was quite diverse with respect to the growth of Christianity. Scholars often place the somewhat Jewish text of the *Didache* in such a setting alongside of the more moderate perspective of the Gospel of Matthew and the extremely liberal views of the bishop Ignatius. The likelihood that three such diverse authors could have written within the same city at roughly the same time indicates the breadth of perspective that the church of Antioch supported.

Much like other ancient cities, Antioch supported a vibrant tradition of time-honored religious sects from Syria, Egypt, and Mesopotamia alongside of the popular emperor cult that had begun to spring up around the Mediterranean basin. But it seems that the presence of the city's large Jewish community led to much of the religious strife that was experienced among area residents. This would explain the Ignatian resistance to the presence of Jewish teachings and traditions within the structure of Christian theology and ecclesiology. Ignatius does not appear to have shared a Jewish background himself. And he found the teachings of Paul to serve as a worthy backdrop to his understanding of the church as a new faith at work within the world. At the same time, however, the continued presence of a large and influential Jewish contingent in the city in subsequent decades would explain why the calls of Ignatius ultimately were left unheeded by the local church, since the late second-century bishops Theophilus and Serapion clearly made concerted efforts to shape the church of Antioch in a way that would appeal to the synagogue. So it seems that the numerous bishops of the city that stretched from the apostle Peter until the third century found that they remained in the continual situation of defining what it meant to be Christian in relationship to the synagogue.

5. Egypt

The history of early Christianity in Egypt is particularly intriguing, though the roots of that tradition remain somewhat murky. There is clear evidence of church activities within the principal city of Alexandria, as well as at a secondary site nearby in Naucratis. Otherwise, it seems that much of Egyptian Christianity spawned from the individual interpretations of local believers about what it meant to be a follower of Christ. In some respects it was this very attitude that led to the great monastic traditions of the Egyptian wilderness that are featured in the exploits of the monks Antony, Pachomius, and Shenoute. The *Apophthegmata Patrum*, an expansive collection of sayings and episodes from the lives of early pious Christians, offers clear evidence of monastic life and teaching in the region. But the great centuries of monastic organization ultimately lie beyond the period of the Apostolic Fathers and thus remain of little concern for our present study.

The more important facet of Egyptian Christianity that must be considered here is the enormous influence that Judaism once more played upon the rise of the institution of the church and its theological speculation. Alexandria, like Antioch, was firmly rooted in a broad Jewish tradition of scholarship and academic training. This was the home of the first Greek translation of the Hebrew Bible, the Septuagint, and of the great Jewish philosopher and theologian, Philo. Both of these forces had great effect upon subsequent Christian thought, most especially in the region of Alexandria. At the same time, Egyptian thinkers were highly influenced by Gnostic interpretations of religious and philosophical principles, a tendency that many scholars see at work behind the thought processes of the letter of *Barnabas*. There is little question that Gnostic speculation typically came to characterize early Christian theology both in Alexandria and throughout Upper Egypt. In many respects, a marriage of Judaism and Gnosticism that was not always present elsewhere among Christians in the first and second centuries served to drive the evolution of the church of Egypt.

It is most curious that the author of Acts tells us nothing about the rise of the church in this region. This may be explained to some extent by the narrative of the text as it carefully follows the experiences of the Jerusalem church to the great missionary journeys of Paul throughout Syria, Asia Minor, Greece, and Italy. In some sense, Acts may provide us only with the limited information about the church that its author had at hand. At the same time, however, one must wonder whether the reconstruction of Christianity's early growth that serves as the basis of Acts reflects a conscious attempt within the early church to excise the historical record with respect to activities within Egypt. There is no question that the idea of Egypt as a theologically suspect region dominated Jewish, and subsequently Christian, thought. We note that one always "goes down to Egypt" within the literature, since it was there that the human spirit and its relationship to God were seen to be most threatened in the eyes of the Judeo-Christian tradition.

Egyptian Christianity ultimately collected itself into the Coptic Orthodox Church as distinct from Roman Catholicism and Greek Orthodoxy. The unique nature of the church in this part of the world struggled to establish its own identity, keeping itself distinct from the growing institutions of Christianity that were forming elsewhere throughout the Roman Empire. The primary apostolic tradition of Egypt is based upon the witness of John Mark, who traveled to Egypt with his gospel message after his encounters with the apostle Peter in Rome. Thus the Egyptian church claimed ancient roots for what became the orthodox standards of Christian theology that circulated in the region. But these standards were very slow to develop over the centuries in the light of competing ideas about what it meant to be Christian.

Of primary influence in the city of Alexandria, apart from the presence of the Greek Old Testament and the speculations of Philo, was the presence of the great Alexandrian library. Renowned as an exceptional center of learning and a repository of ancient texts throughout the Mediterranean world, the library ultimately provided an academic background for early Christian scholars who wished to explore their faith through manuscripts

45

and research. In the light of this repository of ancient wisdom, the scholar Pantaenus established his famous catechetical school, which eventually became the home of later Christian theologians like Clement of Alexandria, Origen, and Didymus the Blind. These scholars worked in Alexandria in an effort to provide a solid theological structure to the framework of Christian theology and to appropriate ethical living. But, of course, the results of their work were not achieved until long after the end of the second century.

What is most instructive about the work of the great Christian thinkers of the third and fourth centuries in Alexandria is the interpretive technique they employed in their work, for they were primarily dependent upon the allegorical interpretation of scripture. This process, which argues that literary texts are not to be read literally but symbolically, had been widely employed by local Jewish scholars. Subsequently, it was only natural that Christians in the region made similar use of the technique. This is perhaps one of the most convincing reasons why scholars assign a text like *Barnabas* to the sphere of Egyptian Christianity, since its author is particularly adept at allegorical methodology. But furthermore, the text of *Barnabas* reveals a close relationship to Jewish history and traditions, which might also be easily assigned to the same region. And finally, the author of *Barnabas* is greatly concerned for the role of Christian knowledge as an element of human salvation, a construct that was typical among many of Alexandria's great ecclesiastical thinkers. Such arguments are certainly not conclusive, of course. But as a cluster of ideas, they are highly reasonable in the light of what we know about the spread of early Christian values and opinions around the Mediterranean world.

In a theological sense, church authorities and theologians around the Roman Empire commonly viewed Egyptian Christianity with a healthy attitude of suspicion. Many later Christians in Egypt were confirmed Arians, and most held to a certain "logos theology" that one now associates with the Gospel of John. Such ideas were particularly difficult for "orthodox" bishops and theologians to address as they attempted to pull together a standard of faith for their local dioceses and, ultimately, for the modern church. The tensions and conflicts that resulted among those who debated such patterns of speculation in northern Egypt often led to violence between ecclesiastical authorities and parishioners. On more than one occasion the local bishop was driven to make use of military force as a means by which to ensure that orthodox standards were followed among the various churches and monasteries that eventually sprang up along the shores of the Nile. Such efforts certainly had mixed results, and the implications that these conflicts held for the relationship between religion and civil society often led to turmoil during the administrations of the emperors Constantine and Theodosius.

Ultimately, the relationship between religion and state was a decisive factor for all Christians around the Mediterranean basin. As various faiths and cults competed for respect in the eyes of Rome, the primary standard by which tolerance was granted was the extent to which individual religions offered cultural and political support to ancient society's standards. The struggle of the early church as it challenged those standards with a new message of freedom in Christ, mixed together with a variety of local, ethnic customs and views, ultimately led to the martyrdom of numerous Christians throughout the world. But the eventual success of the church was assured, as is witnessed by the extent to which it reshaped the very nature of the empire.

CHAPTER 3

Connections to Scripture

The many Christians who produced the works that now appear in the Apostolic Fathers were deeply influenced by the presence of religious literary sources that we now call scripture. But while modern Christians point to a specific list of ancient texts as scripture, writings that have been approved by ecclesiastical authorities through numerous centuries, the earliest followers of Christ worked with a much more fluid concept of what was suitable for use. They needed texts that were appropriate for prayer and liturgy, for meditation and theological speculation, for ethical instruction and ecclesiastical regulation, and as a means by which to test the religious credentials of those who came to their local communities in the name of Christ.

For most early Christians, their Jewish background naturally led them to respect the same literary texts that were widely recognized within the synagogue. Included here were the various writings of the Torah and the Prophets, and to some lesser extent, the so-called Writings. These texts were widely employed by Jews in all places, were recognized as valuable for study and prayer, and were considered to be sound liturgical and ethical guidelines. By the first century C.E., however, many Jews outside of Palestine who could no longer work well with the Hebrew language chose to use a Greek translation of the scriptures. This translation, the

Septuagint, included a handful of texts that were not included in the Hebrew Bible and were generally considered to be more recent works than the Torah, Prophets, and Writings. Thus the canon of scripture became extended for many Jews. And when a number of these Greek-speaking Jews experienced a conversion to Christianity, their expanded canon of authoritative writings seeped into the life of faith that circulated within the early church as well.

With time, of course, an increasing number of early Christians no longer came to the church through the roots of the Jewish tradition, but were converts from various ethnic origins. Many of these believers recognized an even broader range of authoritative writings than those that were endorsed within Judaism. And as they came into contact with fellow Christians of Jewish background, it became clear that works representing the experiences of faith that had been observed within both groups needed to be collected together as a testimony to the common understanding of the wider church. Though this process took several centuries, the final production was what we now recognize as the New Testament.

In the following pages we will make a brief survey of these two primary sets of texts that served as the sources by which early Christians evaluated their faith experiences, the Jewish scriptures (or Old Testament) and the New Testament. We must remember than neither canon was firmly established by the time of the Apostolic Fathers. Further, individual writings within each literary collection held varying importance among our authors, often reflecting each text's sense of dependence either upon the Jewish tradition or, instead, upon the rising authority of early Christian literature.

1. Old Testament Sources

The collected works of the Apostolic Fathers represent a wide diversity of approaches to Judaism's scriptures and cultural traditions. Some authors were clearly steeped in the religious background of Jewish culture and thought, while others seem either to have avoided it or to have attacked it. In the following review of how our texts made use of the Old Testament and its traditions, we begin with those authors who showed either apathy or hostility toward Jewish ideas, offering some explanation for their position. What we discover from the outset is that the Apostolic Fathers are almost evenly divided with respect to this issue.

It seems natural to begin with what is the most recent text in our collection, the *Epistle to Diognetus*. In the first ten chapters of this work there appear to be relatively few allusions to the Old Testament, and these are primarily in the form of stock phrases that circulated widely among Christians. There is certainly no extended explanation of specific texts from Jewish sources.

The situation changes in the final two chapters, however, whose materials preserve part of a separate homily. In this concluding section we find that our author speaks in part about the garden of paradise that was known from Genesis 3. But in reality this passage can hardly be restricted to Jewish interests, since its focus, the rebellion of humanity against God, was widely used by both Jewish and Christian authors alike with little concern for the situation of Judaism itself. Indeed, the problem of religious rebellion is a universal phenomenon, and our author speaks of the situation in just such a manner.

Otherwise throughout *Diognetus* there is no concern for the Old Testament or its themes. This omission seems reasonable to a large extent, since the work, written in the last half of the second century, fell into a period of time after the church had made a clean break with Judaism. More importantly, the author of *Diognetus* seeks to explain Christianity in large part in contrast to the false practices of the synagogue. It may have seemed counterproductive to employ the authoritative texts of Jewish tradition in an effort to discredit Judaism itself. And if this was indeed the perspective of our author, then it seems quite likely that *Diognetus* did not spring from a Jewish heritage, though this remains uncertain.

A second writing to consider here is the *Shepherd of Hermas*. The author of this work has a singular approach to Christian tradition, making little reference either to Jewish scriptures or to any known texts from our New Testament. But this does not completely remove the work from the traditional borders of early Christian literature, since the *Shepherd* taps into long-established biblical themes throughout its teachings. In chapter 36, for example, one discovers a reference to the two angels of righteousness and wickedness who control the actions of humanity. There are parallels to this same "two ways" theme in Deuteronomy and Jeremiah, a motif that is likewise continued in the Gospel of Matthew, the *Didache*, and *Barnabas*. A second Old Testament image appears in chapter 59, where God's people are described as the vineyard of the Lord. This allusion to biblical thought relies upon similar texts in the Psalms and the prophets Isaiah and Ezekiel. Finally, in chapter 92 we discover a text in which the patriarchs and prophets of ancient Israel are described as the foundation stones of the church, depicted here as a tower. Though no explanation of their specific contribution to Christianity is offered, their presence in the process is nonetheless significant. Thus we notice that biblical themes and images are indeed present throughout the *Shepherd*. But while such vestiges of Jewish tradition receive consideration by our author, it is all the more remarkable that the *Shepherd*, the longest of our writings, omits any in-depth examination of specific scriptural passages.

We turn next to the literature that is associated with the figures of the bishops Polycarp and Ignatius. With respect to Polycarp, we have both a letter from the bishop's hand and a personal recollection of his death by one or more of his followers. In neither instance is there a large amount of concern for Jewish tradition or for the Old Testament. This does not actually stand as much of a surprise in the case of the *Martyrdom* perhaps, since our author(s) points toward the Jews as a people who both encouraged the persecution of Polycarp and assisted the Romans in his execution. Much like the late second-century circumstances of *Diognetus*, one might argue that there is a narrative rationale for the omission of Old Testament references here. The use of such texts would have been viewed as counterproductive in an argument against the Jews, the very group of people who are envisioned as violent opponents to Christianity. This motif is quite typical of Christian writings after the early second century.

When we turn to Polycarp's letter to the Philadelphians, we find a set of circumstances that speaks to the situations both of Polycarp and of Ignatius. While these two leaders served as significant influences upon the rise of the church in Asia Minor and Syria respectively, a key element that may have ultimately bound the two bishops together was the likelihood that neither appears to have come from a Jewish heritage. One observes, for example, that neither man's name is based upon Hebrew origins. Furthermore, none of the epistles from either bishop appeals in any extensive way to the Old Testament or to Jewish tradition for its authority. Our single letter by Polycarp makes several oblique references to certain scriptural phrases from the book of Proverbs and the prophecies of Isaiah, Jeremiah, and Tobit. But these texts were widely known and commonly employed among early Christians and probably were available to the bishop from the universal background of customary church usage.

All the more remarkable is the situation of Ignatius. Though highly dependent upon a variety of sources for his many arguments, he cites the Old Testament only three times, twice from Proverbs and once from Isaiah. Otherwise, he makes only a few scattered allusions to materials in the Psalms, Judges, and Deuteronomy, but not in any particularly significant way. We must question whether Ignatius was actually very familiar with the Old Testament.[1] Anyone with a solid knowledge of Judaism's literary tradition could have made ample use of numerous scriptural texts and themes to add fortitude to the arguments that Ignatius offered to his readers. At the same time, however, one might argue that Ignatius was in the same situation as the authors of *Diognetus* and the *Martyrdom*. Like those writers, Ignatius would not have been interested to draw upon texts that might otherwise be associated with a group against which he wrote. In this case it was not the Jews specifically, but the so-called Judaizers who wished to shape Christianity according to Jewish customs and practices. It is perhaps this second reason, an avoidance of too many Old Testament images, that ultimately seems most persuasive in the case of Ignatius. Hence, we find that some of the most diverse texts within the Apostolic Fathers—the letters of Ignatius and Polycarp, and the writings of *Diognetus* and the *Martyrdom*—may have avoided both Old Testament usages and Jewish traditions for the same reason, in order to avoid any association with their opponents from the synagogue.

We are left with several writings from the Apostolic Fathers that make quite specific use of Old Testament texts for somewhat different reasons through a variety of approaches. These writings include *1–2 Clement*, the *Didache*, and *Barnabas*. It is perhaps not by accident that the majority (if not all) of these works should be counted among the earliest of our writings. In many respects their authors were in touch with churches that remained in close contact either with the synagogue or with Christians of Jewish background. And if we can accept the locations for each text as presented in chapter 1, we might find that each author wrote within a setting that was alive with Jews and Jewish Christians, namely, Rome, Corinth, Antioch, and Alexandria. But not all of these authors were sympathetic to Jewish ideas and customs. Indeed, the letter of *Barnabas* actually employs Old Testament texts and imagery as a means by which to attack Judaism. Since this hostility to the synagogue dovetails with the works that we have discussed above, it is to the text of *Barnabas* that we turn next.

The text of *Barnabas* is an intriguing piece within the Apostolic Fathers by virtue of its consistent use of Old Testament passages and images. There are constant references to the "Law and the Prophets," and specific usages of a variety of individual Jewish authors. Included here are citations from Genesis, Psalms, and Deuteronomy, and numerous references to passages from Isaiah, Jeremiah, and Zechariah. Such works ultimately come to form the basis of the many biblical images that appear throughout the narrative of *Barnabas*. Key themes include concepts such as the idea of sacrifice and the significance of the stone on which the faith of Israel was set, the role of circumcision in the family of the church, the importance of the Sabbath, and the responsibility of Christians as heirs of salvation in relationship to their Savior, the Son of David.

While the author of *Barnabas* makes use of a considerable number of scriptural texts and themes, the sources from which they are drawn are actually clustered around only a few key biblical books. This clustering effect has suggested to numerous scholars that our author made extensive use of ancient "testimonia," early collections of biblical passages that were gathered around specific motifs of special interest to the early church. In the case of *Barnabas* these collections would have been oriented primarily toward the concept of salvation and the role of Christ in the transference of God's covenant relationship with the Jews toward a similar affiliation with Christians. And this seems to stand as the most interesting aspect of our author's use of scripture, that is, the

54

adaptation of Judaism's own authoritative texts as a witness against the claims of the Jewish community to be the covenant people of God. The text of *Barnabas* is replete with examples of how the Old Testament witnesses to Judaism's misappropriation of its privileged status under the covenant, thereby shirking its responsibilities to God in specific and to humanity in general. It is Israel's disobedience to God, its inability to follow the divine Law, and its rejection of God's Messiah who was sent for the salvation of all people that our author finds foreshadowed throughout the Old Testament.

This adaptation of the Jewish scriptures for the purpose of attacking Judaism is a novel approach among the Apostolic Fathers. It is certainly not paralleled in texts like *Diognetus* and the *Martyrdom*, or in the letters of Ignatius, even though these particular authors had clearly directed much of their religious anger toward the synagogue, which had rejected the early church. Indeed, there are elements about *Barnabas* that make it unique in comparison to the efforts of these other writers. In the first place, *Barnabas* makes extensive use of the allegorical method of interpretation in order to give new meaning to older texts. The reader is offered innovative ways of viewing scriptural passages in a Christian light, redefining texts that had long been translated according to strict norms of Jewish interpretation. Secondly, the intimate association that *Barnabas* seems to share with Judaism's scriptures and interpretive methodology suggest that its author came from a Jewish background. Admittedly, our writer is now an uncompromising advocate of Christian ideas and views of salvation. Yet this perspective may easily be explained as the result of our author's status as a recent convert. Thus we find that the perspective of *Barnabas* with reference to the Old Testament and Jewish tradition differs markedly from that of our previous authors.

We turn next to the three texts that seem to be most accepting of Old Testament passages and their traditional interpretations. Primary among these writings is the *Didache*. The first third of the *Didache* is oriented around the theme of life and death that we have identified above as the "two ways" motif. We have already seen this Old Testament idea at work in the *Shepherd* under the labels of righteousness (= life) and wickedness (= death). Parallel materials are also to be found in *Barnabas* 18–20. The *Didache* is unique among the Apostolic Fathers with respect to its presentation of this motif, however, by virtue of the manner in which it approaches the materials. While the way of death is encapsulated in a brief, concluding list of sins that are widely documented elsewhere throughout Jewish and Hellenistic literature alike, the way of life has received a decidedly Jewish interpretation. Indeed, the reader is instructed to think of the way of life as a fulfillment of the Ten Commandments, given to Moses by God on Mount Sinai and now preserved in Exodus and Deuteronomy. The various laws that are found there—do not murder, do not commit adultery, do not steal, etc.—become the framework of ethical living around which Christians may be assured of correct thought and practice. But in addition to this structure, the reader is encouraged to avoid certain other sinful actions and inclinations that may themselves lead to unintentional transgressions against the Ten Commandments. For example, we are told not to corrupt youth, not to practice magic, not to engage in sorcery, and so forth, for such actions lead to murder, adultery, theft, etc. Scholars recognize this process as a typical Jewish technique by which warnings against lesser temptations are provided as a means by which to protect God's followers from committing more significant sins.

We see this process identified elsewhere in the New Testament Gospels with respect to the scribes and Pharisees, two religious parties that were known for having established an "oral Law" around the written Law. This protection maintained the purity of God's commandments against humanity's tendency toward sin. The Didachist, like the scribes and Pharisees, employs this same process in the production of the "two ways," indicating the presence of Jewish attitudes intermingled with Christian concerns.

Also in the *Didache*, there is a heavy dependence upon other themes and images from the Jewish scriptures. By way of example, our author expounds upon the way of life through a teaching technique of the wisdom tradition, that is, by making repeated reference to the reader as "my child." This same approach is commonly employed in the book of Proverbs. In addition, a variety of scriptural sources are incorporated throughout the narrative, including passages from Exodus, Leviticus, and Deuteronomy, the prophets Isaiah, Zechariah, and Malachi, the wisdom instruction of Sirach, and the Psalms. But our author is not restricted to the use of literary sources alone. In fact, the *Didache* is highly dependent upon a variety of Jewish traditions for the composition of its liturgical and ecclesiastical materials. Thus we note the insistence that readers baptize in "living water" (= running water), a practice that was prescribed by rabbinic tradition. And quite specific prayers are presented for use during the ritual of the Eucharist, words that clearly have their source in Jewish mealtime prayers that were commonly spoken by Jews during the observance of Passover. The *Didache* is quite unique among early Christian writings for its decided incorporation of such specific Jewish approaches to important church rituals. It seems evident that our author was in open contact with the traditions of the synagogue and respected the authority that Judaism's cultic practices held for the correct observance of acceptable worship. There is little question that the *Didache* preserves our closest link to Christianity's Jewish roots from among the texts that have been preserved within the Apostolic Fathers.

Finally, we turn to our last two texts, the letter of *1 Clement* and the ancient Christian homily that is preserved in *2 Clement*. The author of each text has made some limited use of Old Testament passages and themes, each reflecting an appreciation for the authoritative images of Jewish tradition.

The author of *1 Clement* seems to be aware of a broad range of materials from the Old Testament. Included among the materials that appear here are passages from Genesis, Exodus, Numbers, Deuteronomy, Joshua, 1 Samuel, Esther, Job, Psalms, Proverbs, Isaiah, Jeremiah, and Ezekiel, as well as the works of Judith, the Wisdom of Solomon, and Sirach from the Apocrypha. It is quite possible that *1 Clement*, like *Barnabas*, has employed some form of "testimonia" as a source for these references. But unlike *Barnabas*, our author has gleaned from such a broad variety of texts that this option seems less likely in this case. Furthermore, the construction of *1 Clement* suggests that our author is intimately familiar both with literary sources and a variety of oral traditions by which to interpret them. One might argue that this familiarity with interpretive techniques stems from the close relationship between the church and Judaism that existed in ancient Rome. But this remains uncertain.

The most intriguing aspect of the way in which *1 Clement* applies texts from the Jewish scriptures may be found in the close association that the author draws between typical Christian themes and specific biblical figures. For example, our author borrows from Genesis, Exodus, Numbers, and 1 Samuel to demonstrate how jealousy creates division within community life, focusing upon the broken relationships that resulted from the bitterness between Cain and Abel, Jacob and Esau, Moses and Pharaoh, Aaron and Miriam, Dathan and Abiram, and David and Saul. In a similar manner, the books of Genesis, Jonah, Joshua, Job, and Psalms are employed in order to indicate a series of actions and attitudes that led Judaism's forefathers toward salvation, including repentance (so Noah and Jonah), obedience (so Enoch), faith (so Abraham and Isaac), and humility (so Abraham, Jacob, Laban, and David). And most importantly, the author of *1 Clement* makes explicit use of passages that indicate the strong leadership qualities of Moses, who enabled the people of Israel to survive as they struggled in their wilderness flight from Egypt toward the Promised Land. As envisioned from the witnesses of Exodus, Numbers, and Deuteronomy, Moses is offered as God's prototype for all people of faith, someone who represents the ideal of what leaders within the church should themselves seek to imitate. The consistent use of themes and images from Judaism's literary tradition clearly indicates our author's comfort with Jewish traditions and texts, not just because they have been the elements of choice from the perspective of the author, but because they were deemed to be suitable as tools by which to direct and motivate the church in Corinth as well.

The author of *2 Clement* is also comfortable with Jewish texts and themes, but in another way. The most significant difference here is the close attention that our author provides to a single passage of scripture, Isaiah 54. It is perhaps to be expected that a homily would be designed around an individual text from scripture. And the use of materials from the prophets was certainly a favorite approach among early Christians, especially the writings of Isaiah, Jeremiah, and Ezekiel. One discovers a similar dependence upon the oracles of the prophets among the writers of the New Testament. At the same time, *2 Clement* has employed this framework from Isaiah as the foundation by which to incorporate numerous other passages from the Old Testament, including reflections of Genesis, Proverbs, Jeremiah, Ezekiel, and Malachi. There is a certain ease and fluidity in this manipulation of scripture that suggests the amazing degree to which our author was comfortable with the material, not as a tool by which to assault Judaism and Jewish issues, but as an instrument of interpretation through which the church could come to see itself in contrast to the imagery of ancient Israel.

Thus we find that the writings of the Apostolic Fathers, texts that cover a period of roughly a century of early Christian experience, reflect a variety of responses toward the presence of Judaism and its traditions. For the authors of the *Didache* and *1–2 Clement*, Jewish sources continued to serve as the foundation of many Christian hopes and aspirations. For other authors like Polycarp and Ignatius, as well as the authors of the *Martyrdom* and *Diognetus*, the Old Testament was primarily viewed as a deterrent to valid faith. Finally, to the author of the *Shepherd* the Jewish heritage was seen as essential to the rise of Christianity, but not particularly worthy of exploration. Perhaps the most intriguing element of such early patristic views of Judaism and the Old Testament is the lack of a consistent approach that developed over time. Earlier texts were divided over their use of Jewish scriptures, as were later works. The Apostolic Fathers had a great influence over how the Old Testament was viewed by early Christians; these texts became significant in the struggle between church and synagogue.

2. New Testament Sources

Attempts to determine how the Apostolic Fathers have made use of writings that now form the New Testament are complicated by a series of factors. From the outset, many of our writers were active during the same period of time that much Christian scripture itself was written. The authors of the *Didache* and *1 Clement*, and perhaps even *Barnabas*, lived and wrote during the same approximate time period as the production of many of the New Testament Gospels, the book of Acts, the so-called Pastoral Epistles (1–2 Timothy and Titus), Revelation, 1–3 John, 2 Peter, and perhaps Hebrews. This means that the world in which these authors lived was essentially the same with respect to the historical development of the church. Other authors from the Apostolic Fathers, writers such as Ignatius and Polycarp, and perhaps the author of the *Shepherd*, were active only a short time thereafter.

A second consideration is the confusion that is caused by the fact that the Apostolic Fathers and New Testament have both made extensive use of the Old Testament. This often leads to the problem of whether an author in the Apostolic Fathers has drawn from a New Testament text that is quoting from an Old Testament source or, instead, has quoted directly from the Old Testament source itself. In many situations it is simply impossible to answer this question with satisfaction. The early church shaped a large portion of its self-identity around the Jewish scriptures, having incorporated them into early Christian liturgy and ethical instructions. Sayings that reflect traditional Jewish wisdom and popular religious images that are based upon the insights of Israel's great tradition of prophets very quickly managed to weave themselves into the literature of the ancient church. In many instances it is quite difficult to separate the sources of such materials from the Christian editors who incorporated those texts into their own works. At the same time, however, the various ways in which early Christian authors have made use of their Jewish sources often indicates the unique nature of the church's early faith as it sought to adapt ideas and images into a new perspective of belief.

Let us begin with the figures of Ignatius and Polycarp, who were among the earliest of our Apostolic Fathers to incorporate the growing influence of earlier Christian leaders. As we have seen above, neither of these bishops seems to have made extensive use of Old Testament sources. In part, they may have been uncomfortable with Jewish texts and traditions and, in part, they may have found such materials to be poor tools as they resisted early Christian groups that sought to return the church to its Jewish roots. At the same time, however, it seems that both of these men were highly influenced by the literary efforts of the apostle Paul, who held as a key element of his missionary work the need for Christians to break free from the cultic and legalistic restrictions by which the synagogue had entangled those who followed the Jewish faith. Both Ignatius and Polycarp appear to have held Paul as something of a religious icon. And when they heard the apostle argue for the need to break free from Jewish restrictions, they interpreted that to mean the necessity of the church to break from Judaism itself.

This interpretation of Paul's teachings ultimately came to dominate the tide of the early church's self-understanding. And for leaders such as Ignatius and Polycarp, Paul became the model upon which the argument was waged. This appears very clearly in the works of Ignatius, who patterned his letters upon parallel Pauline texts that are now contained in the New Testament. The best example of his dependence upon Paul appears in the Ignatian letter to Rome, where the bishop's opening praise of Roman Christianity appears to be a direct reflection of the introductory materials that appear in the apostle's own letter to the city. Such high praise serves as a special connection between these two works for several reasons. In the first instance, neither Paul nor Ignatius began any other letter with such words or in such a manner. Secondly, neither author had visited the city of Rome previously to our knowledge, yet both approach the church with the same attitude, that is, the stance that a client would take with respect to a patron. In other words, though neither man seems to have had a direct relationship with the church at Rome, each opted to place himself in the position of humility, as someone who can only ask for favors, not demand action. In the case of Paul, he asks the divergent factions of the church in Rome to respect one another and to accept the theology that he endorses. In the case of Ignatius, he requests that the Roman church not use its power of influence with the imperial government to save him from the martyrdom that he anticipates will crown his achievements as a worthy disciple of Christ.

Ignatius makes similar use of Pauline materials when he writes to the church at Ephesus. Clearly aware the Ephesians had spent some considerable amount of time with Paul when the apostle had visited the city some half century previously, Ignatius patterns his letter there upon the framework of the text of Ephesians that now is preserved in our New Testament. This is particularly intriguing in that, while Ignatius often employs various Pauline imagery throughout his letters, his actual letter form rarely follows Paul's somewhat unique style, except in this single instance. But we must not forget that scholars often reject the authenticity of the New Testament letter to the Ephesians, attributing it instead to one of Paul's devoted followers. This suggests that Ignatius has composed his own letter to Ephesus based upon his close association with some Pauline school of thought, typical of Christians who were oriented toward Pauline ideas and theology.

We should probably also include Polycarp in such a category, since he too is highly dependent upon Pauline imagery in his letter. There are even scholars of early church history who have argued that the Pastoral Epistles of the New Testament, which are often credited to a student of Paul and not to the apostle himself, were actually written by the bishop Polycarp late in the first century.[2] Indeed, we must always be aware of the influence that important early church figures like Ignatius and Polycarp undoubtedly had as they worked to expand the influence of the ancient church. Their contributions to early Christian literature and thought may extend far beyond the more obvious texts that remain from their hand.

This brings us to a consideration of specific literary forms that appear throughout the New Testament and the Apostolic Fathers. These may easily be divided into two groups: general categories and specific materials. As to the latter, there are numerous sayings that have been utilized by the authors of our collection that have exact or close parallels among the texts of the New Testament. While it is certainly not possible to review these in their entirety here, I shall address the more important of them momentarily. For now, however, we will survey some of the general literary forms that span our two collections, forms that include instructional codes, apocalyptic materials, liturgical sources, and so forth.

With respect to instructional materials, the New Testament makes use of several primary forms of ethical instruction, primarily including so-called "virtue-vice lists" and household codes. Virtue-vice lists typically are lengthy registers of actions and motivations grouped either into a category of acceptable behavior or unacceptable conduct. Thus we find such lists occasionally offered by Jesus in the Gospels when he is asked to define the nature of life in the kingdom of God. But much more often we see both Paul and the authors of the Pastoral Epistles and 1–2 Peter make extensive use of such lists as the criteria by which Christians can reassure themselves that they are worthy to enter the kingdom itself.

An excellent example may be found in Galatians 5:19-21:

> Now the works of the flesh are plain: fornication, impurity, licentiousness, idolatry, sorcery, enmity, strife, jealousy, anger, selfishness, dissension, party spirit, envy, drunkenness, carousing, and the like. (RSV)

In the same way, writers such as Ignatius and Polycarp and the authors of *1 Clement*, the *Didache*, and *Barnabas* incorporate similar lists into their definitions of the ethical Christian lifestyle. This type of approach to religious instruction was widely used among both early Jews and members of non-Jewish religions. Within Judaism, such lists were often oriented around the Ten Commandments in an effort to bring customary teachings in line with biblical doctrine, as we have seen in the *Didache* above.

Another instructional form that was popular during our period was that of the household codes. These codes were drawn from the standard model by which both families and institutions came to organize themselves in Greek and Roman society. Of primary importance in this effort was the delineation of offices and functions. Thus, typical codes specified the ways in which husbands and wives were to treat one another, the means by which parents and children were to relate, and the standards that masters and servants were to follow as they conducted their affairs. Each person was defined according to his or her role within the family and society, and each was expected to act appropriately in that position. It is particularly interesting that such codes are never used in the teachings of Jesus or in the instructions of Paul. On the other hand, those New Testament authors who wrote in the tradition of Paul, or in response to him, made considerable use of this pedagogical form. We see such codes in the Pastoral Epistles and 1 Peter, for example. In addition, several are preserved in the *Didache* and in the letters of Ignatius and Polycarp. There is little question that the early church found household codes to serve as a useful form of organization for Christian culture. With the eventual rise of a system of monarchial bishops and standard ecclesiastical administration throughout the churches in the middle of the second century, however, the use of household codes virtually disappeared from early Christian literature. Undoubtedly, when their presence became a distraction to the personal authority of church leaders, they were deemed to be unimportant for ethics and theology. For the late first century and early second century, however, household codes clearly were seen as advantageous.

This brings us to apocalyptic literature. The nature of apocalyptic texts is both to reveal the previously unknown and to motivate the reader toward some ethical behavior. This category tends to appear in general ways throughout the New Testament and can easily be found in texts like Mark 13, 1 Thessalonians, and Revelation. The Gospel of Matthew incorporates the apocalyptic materials of Mark into chapters 23–24, but generally employs scattered apocalyptic sayings throughout. In the Apostolic Fathers we find that the *Didache* concludes with a chapter that reflects New Testament apocalyptic materials. So too, the opening visions of the *Shepherd* employ the figure of a great beast, much like the book of Revelation. And *Barnabas*, like Matthew, offers apocalyptic connections with Daniel in an attempt to motivate its readers toward an appropriate response to God's new covenant in the church. A similar trend appears throughout the letters of Ignatius, though he makes far less use of the theme as a motivation for his readers.

Another literary type that permeates the Apostolic Fathers is that of liturgical materials. This is perhaps most evident in the *Didache*, whose author makes reference to baptismal procedures, appropriate prayer, the correct manner in which to hold Eucharist, and the suitable mind-set in which to worship God. While most of the passages that preserve these liturgical instructions do not have direct literary parallels to writings in the New Testament, the *Didache* does preserve a form of the Lord's Prayer that looks very much like that which appears in Matthew 6.[3] Otherwise, the *Didache* seems to offer two elements to our consideration of early Christian liturgy that either supplement or complement the New Testament. The Didachist tends to offer a specifically Jewish perspective on what was considered to be appropriate liturgical practice within the early church. Scholars have often argued that this tendency indicates that the *Didache* reflects practices that were outside of the mainstream church tradition, perhaps used by some isolated, rural community that was out of step with the broad evolution of early Christian ritual. This need not be the case, however, particularly if the *Didache* represents some of the oldest of early

Christian liturgical practices prior to the influence of non-Jewish elements. At the same time, the Didachist tends to offer "exceptions" to strict liturgical guidelines, observing for example that while baptism should be performed in running water, it need not always be the case. And further, fasting prior to baptism is required only of those who are in a position to do so, not necessarily by all.[4] And of course, while the Didachist insists upon certain guidelines with respect to the appropriate observation of the Eucharist, true prophets are permitted to observe the ritual in whatever way that they deem to be appropriate.

Outside of the *Didache* the question of liturgical elements is primarily restricted to the works of Ignatius. Ignatius was less concerned with the structure of liturgical rituals and more with the theology that stood behind them. We find, for example, that he explains the need for Christian baptism through a unique interpretation of the baptism of Jesus. As Ignatius argues, Jesus was baptized in order to cleanse the water for subsequent Christian baptism.[5] Furthermore, Jesus received a special ointment upon his head, presumably in anticipation of the anointing process within the early church. But once again, the ointment was given to Jesus as a means by which he could breathe incorruptibility into the church. Ignatius also insists that Christians only eat "Christian food" and not the food of heresy.[6] We must presume by this reference that he refers to appropriate elements of the Eucharist, bread and wine that is offered within the security of a doctrinally sound community of faith. Finally, Ignatius warns his readers against continuing with the false liturgical practices of Judaism, rituals that he associates with "strange doctrines or antiquated myths."[7] For him, true Christians must experience the new liturgy of faith in Christ. Indeed, participation in the body of Christ requires that all believers experience an appropriate approach to worship and adoration of God.

We turn now to specific New Testament texts that are reflected throughout the Apostolic Fathers. Once again the *Didache* seems to provide the clearest example of such usages. Scholars have long observed that the many sayings of Jesus that appear in the *Didache* have their closest parallels in the Gospel of Matthew. One finds here, for example, the saying on the "two ways," a reference to the Trinitarian formula in association with baptism, the Lord's Prayer (as seen above), a command not to give holy items to dogs, a promise that the meek will inherit the earth, and so forth. It is not entirely clear that the Didachist has drawn these materials from Matthew itself. Indeed, scholars are divided here. Some prefer the traditional view that the *Didache* has used Matthew as a source. Others now argue that both the Didachist and the author of Matthew have drawn upon common community traditions. And a small minority argue that the *Didache* itself was a source that was used by Matthew or, perhaps, that the two writings evolved through completely independent traditions. Whatever the historical situation may have actually been, the *Didache* stands as persuasive evidence that texts other than those that now appear in the New Testament contained valid teachings that were associated with the name of Jesus. The presence of such literature provides us with an intriguing link to early church interpretations of the Christian good news message that stood outside of the process of canonization.

Apart from the *Didache*, we turn once again to Ignatius and Polycarp. As noted above, these two bishops incorporated numerous images from the teachings of Paul into their letters. Ignatius, for example, incorporates a call to be steadfast and enduring, much as is found in the deuteroPauline letters to the Colossians and Ephesians. He questions the nature of wisdom and appeals to the mysteries of God, clearly reflecting the arguments of 1 Corinthians. Otherwise, he speaks of Christ as the High Priest of the Holy of Holies, an acknowledgment of the theology of Hebrews. Throughout the writings of Ignatius there are hints of themes and images from the Gospel of John. But like the *Didache*, Ignatius seems to be most dependent upon the arguments of Matthew as his primary gospel source. This is a gospel that he rarely quotes directly, but that he seems to presume behind the comments that he offers to his readers.

Polycarp seems to be equally dependent upon Paul in his letters, employing various Pauline themes associated with endurance and faithfulness. And like Ignatius, Polycarp reflects some knowledge of Matthean concerns, speaking in large part to the necessity of righteousness within the church community, a motif that is especially emphasized in Matthew's Sermon on the Mount. There is little question that the two bishops were largely influenced by the same New Testament authors and themes, presumably because of their relatively close geographical proximity and the nature of what the church was becoming in the region of Syria and Asia Minor.

Another interesting reflection of gospel themes and ideas is preserved in the *Martyrdom of Polycarp*. Scholars have often noted the close parallel of names and events between the New Testament Gospels and the *Martyrdom*. For example, Polycarp enters Smyrna on a donkey, offers a prayer for the church, serves as the host for his final meal, is betrayed by a man who is close to him, is interrogated by someone named Herod and by a proconsul, experiences the call of the Jews for his death, is martyred on a Friday, and the remnants of his corpse are taken away by his followers. It is most informative that these scriptural parallels are not all drawn from the same Gospel narrative, but reflect a variety of biblical traditions. This suggests that the editor of the text undoubtedly endeavored to portray the bishop's *Martyrdom* against the known traditions of the New Testament Gospels. When one considers the late date of the work, that is, the latter half of the second century, it is quite probable that our Gospels were all in wide circulation at the time of writing. In either case, the martyrdom of Polycarp became a standard model by which later martyrologies were penned, recounting the deaths of others who remained faithful to Christ through the witness of Polycarp himself.

Elsewhere throughout the Apostolic Fathers there is a scattered witness to the writings of the New Testament. As one might expect, later works tend to offer more awareness of the Christian scriptures. The text of *2 Clement* is typical of this process. The author of this work makes reference to the Christian's knowledge of God and the need to compete in the "immortal contest" of faith, citing texts from 1 Corinthians. There is also a clear dependence upon Paul's use of images about the potter and his clay, the body as the temple of Christ, and the freedom that comes through the gospel message. Early in *2 Clement* one finds an early hymnic fragment that seems to reflect parallels that are preserved in Philippians 2, Hebrews 1, and the prologue of the Gospel of John. Various references to materials that appear in the Gospels of Matthew and Luke also arise throughout the text.

Similar to *2 Clement*, the author of the *Epistle to Diognetus* makes extensive use of Pauline images that have been drawn from

1 Corinthians. There is also a heavy dependence upon the theology of the Gospel of John and 1 John within the writing. This theology tends to focus upon the role of Christ as the Word of God, the nature of Christian knowledge, and the function of God's revelation as it guided the developing church experience. *Diognetus* is a solid witness to the gradual acceptance of Johannine thought and theology as it circulated among Christian churches toward the end of the second century.

Finally, we turn to the *Shepherd of Hermas*. In many respects the teachings that are preserved here reflect ideas from the books of James and 1 Peter. When one compares this to scholarly observations that another text from Rome, *1 Clement*, also was aware of the book of Hebrews, one comes to suspect that such New Testament writings had gained a wide circulation within the church by the early second century, at least within the circle of Rome's Christians. What is most intriguing about the text of the *Shepherd* is that while there are numerous early Christian themes throughout the work that reflect parallel ideas in the New Testament, there are actually precious few citations of biblical texts. This might suggest that our author was not well informed with respect to biblical sources. But it is actually much more likely that the materials that have been secondarily shaped to form the *Shepherd* were themselves quite old within the tradition. And furthermore, these materials undoubtedly developed outside of the primary influence of biblical literature, offering a witness to early Christian writers who were not greatly influenced by Jewish literature and ideas.

It is clear that the authors of the Apostolic Fathers were well versed with respect to their literary sources, including both Old Testament texts and the literature of what was to become the New Testament. Most prominent among these sources seem to have been the Psalms and the prophets of ancient Israel. And from a Christian perspective, both Paul and the Gospel of Matthew were dominant influences for our authors. One also finds key themes from the tradition of Moses as preserved in the Torah and from Johannine literature. The presence of biblical literature and scriptural imagery served to help our authors in the shaping and presentation of their individual theologies, the elements of which will be reviewed in the next chapter.

CHAPTER 4

Theological Ideas

A s with most literature from Christian history, it is important that we understand specific theological views that were held by individual authors as they wrote. We find that this task is especially difficult with respect to the Apostolic Fathers. For while our texts were written within a span of only a century, a variety of theological positions span the corpus. Several factors help to explain this great diversity of perspectives. In the first place, our authors wrote during some of the earliest years of church history. Most of them produced their works within the so-called "post-apostolic age," that is, immediately after the time of the apostles who traveled with Jesus of Nazareth. This period served as a melting pot of theological views, each of which struggled to gain acceptance within the church as it gradually formed itself into an institution of faith.

A second consideration is the fact that our authors, important leaders of the church, likely wrote in different locations to scattered faith communities around the Mediterranean basin. This means that the Christians who wrote our works most likely came from a variety of ethical backgrounds and faith traditions. This diversity is clearly evident in the texts themselves, some of which reflect a strong consciousness of Jewish life and culture and some of which resist that same tradition.

69

We must also consider the intention of each author in the production of individual texts. Our writers were not particularly concerned to explain the details of the theological views that they held. Instead, it is up to us to examine each writing in the collection with an eye toward the theological framework that underpins its argument. And in this process we must be careful not to force any author into agreement with particular New Testament views that we hold dear or into a false harmony with other writers from the Apostolic Fathers.

1. Theology (God)

Mainline Christian tradition has come to confess that God is present in three persons: Father, Son, and Holy Spirit. This Trinitarian formula has been widely accepted in one form or another within the church since the early patristic period. Yet the development of the doctrine was a slow and painful process in which Christians from Egypt to Asia Minor to Greece to Italy were forced to wrestle with the question of how a single God could appear in more than one form and yet not actually exist as multiple deities.

The writings of the Apostolic Fathers are both united and divided on the Trinitarian nature of God. They are united in their belief that the God of Christian faith was to be found in various forms. But they were divided on the way in which those forms should be understood. In many respects this reflects a parallel reality to the process that is at work within the New Testament. For example, while many New Testament authors speak of God as Father in certain situations, or reflect upon either the human or divine nature of Christ as known through Jesus of Nazareth, or describe the work of the Holy Spirit within the Christian community, it is extremely rare to find formal Trinitarian language expressed in a single phrase. Indeed, among our Gospels it is only the author of Matthew who refers to "the name of the Father and of the Son and of the Holy Spirit," this appearing at the end of the Gospel text where Jesus instructs his apostles to go forth and make disciples, baptizing and teaching as he had instructed.[1] Otherwise, our biblical authors do not offer such a clear expression of the Trinitarian formula. They typically refer to the work of God as the Father, or they focus upon the nature of Christ as the Son or the Word of God, or they speak of the Holy Spirit as one who provides special gifts to the believing Christian. But rarely are all of these natures of God brought into association with one another in a specific sense.

The same holds true within the Apostolic Fathers. As one might expect, those authors who are highly dependent upon Jewish traditions and the Hebrew scriptures make continual reference to God in the person of the Father. This is evident, for example, in the texts of *1 Clement* and *Barnabas*, two writings that continually draw upon Jewish texts as the basis for their arguments. The author of *1 Clement* refers to both the communities in Rome and in Corinth as "the church of God" and speaks of Christians as "those chosen by God." The text refers to the "laws of God," the necessity of "fear of God," and the "promises of God" that Christians will eventually inherit as their portion of salvation. It is God who demands Christian obedience, is merciful in all things, and chooses those who are righteous. Likewise, *Barnabas* is highly focused upon God as Father and Savior. It is God who undertakes righteous acts, desires all persons to live as perfect temples of worship, and hates all activity that is evil in nature. All of these images are highly dependent upon Jewish scripture and draw upon specific biblical passages for support.

But our authors do not stop with the image of God the Father, of course. Their view of God's nature extends beyond the traditional monotheistic boundaries of Jewish tradition. We find in *Barnabas* that God was revealed in a Son whose arrival was predicted in the earliest of Judaism's sacred texts, the Torah. Here we are told that God spoke to the Son at the creation of the world, much as an actor would address his or her audience: "Let us make humanity according to our image and likeness . . . "[2] And the Son of God is identified by name as the Lord, whose role at the end of time is to judge the living and the dead. Such descriptions of Christ reflect a very exalted understanding of the Son, a perspective that identifies the Son with the Creator (and Father) in function, if not necessarily in essence.

First Clement offers a parallel development of the image of Christ, referring to "our Lord Christ Jesus" as God's majestic

71

scepter, despised by humanity's weakness but lifted up by God for humanity's salvation.[3] Otherwise, *1 Clement* notes that God's compassionate mercies are available to those who seek them through Jesus Christ, who will be raised as the first fruit of the coming resurrection. This is the same Jesus Christ who is the "High Priest" of human offerings and stands as the guardian and defender of human weaknesses.[4]

Finally, *1 Clement* makes some limited use of the image of the Holy Spirit, particularly in the role of divine wisdom as found in the Hebrew scriptures. It is through the Spirit that Christ calls all believers to come and listen and to learn how to fear the Lord. It is with the firm assurance that is provided by the Holy Spirit that the good news may be preached throughout the world. And it was through the Spirit that the Holy Scriptures were given.

This use of Spirit imagery in *1 Clement* is particularly interesting for several reasons. In the first place, what is said about the Holy Spirit as the conveyor of the wisdom tradition finds fitting parallels in Jewish sources. At the beginning of Genesis we see that God creates the world through the breath (or spirit) that is breathed across the waters of the deep. The author of the Gospel of John taps into this same imagery in the opening prologue of the Gospel text, indicating that "the Word" was present at the creation and was the avenue through which all things were created. But the author of John means more than what is implied in Genesis, intending to call upon the developing Jewish belief that the figure of Wisdom, who speaks as a personified voice in the book of Proverbs, was present at the creation of the world. Thus it is that the one, holy God, who (according to late Jewish theologians) eventually was viewed as too sacred to be in direct contact with the soiled world in which humanity lived, was viewed as the Creator who fashioned the world through the agency of Wisdom. This idea that God acted through a divine agent is now endorsed in the image of the Word of God that permeates the theology of the Gospel of John and is represented both by the figures of the Son and of the Holy Spirit.

In the second place, the role of the Holy Spirit was not addressed extensively in the literature of the second-century church. Indeed, church councils only considered the place of the Spirit within the divine Trinity at a much later date. The reason for this omission was probably twofold. Second-century theologians found themselves preoccupied with discussions about the relationship of the Son to the Father, both in terms of essence and function. Early Christians experienced great tension over the question of how Jesus as the Christ could be divine alongside of the Father without stretching the strict monotheism of their Jewish heritage beyond rationality. At the same time, numerous early Christian groups had laid claim to the presence of the Spirit as a motivator for their liturgical eccentricities and prophetic rituals. The place of the Spirit and prophecy in the early church were exceedingly difficult to control as Christians attempted to establish working models of power. Thus, the extended discussion of such elements was generally shunned as a danger to church order and hierarchy.

The single exception to this perspective in the Apostolic Fathers is found in the *Shepherd of Hermas*, which depicts the Spirit in the guise of numerous female virgins. These women assist in the construction of the church and are ultimately sent home with the hero of the text, Hermas, to live with him and keep his household faithful and orderly. While we are told that the relationship between Hermas and the Spirits was pure and was directed toward the worship of God, one can easily understand how such speculation made early Christian theologians uneasy.

Certain authors among the Apostolic Fathers hold widely disparate views with respect to the nature of the Christ. At one end of this perspective, the *Didache* never makes any explicit link between Jesus and his divine nature. The divine authority behind the text's sayings and liturgical instructions is simply called "the Lord," leaving the definition of that source to the inclinations of the reader. Is "the Lord" intended to be God the Father, Jesus the human teacher, or Jesus Christ as the Son of God? It is true that, alone among the Apostolic Fathers, it is only the Didachist who uses the Trinitarian formula, a phrase that may have entered the text under the influence of Matthew.[5] But otherwise, the Christology of the *Didache* is generally classified as quite "low," that is, it holds little concern for the divine nature of Jesus as the Christ.

With respect to the other end of the debate, we turn to *2 Clement*, which begins with the words: "We ought to consider

Jesus Christ as we do God—judge of the living and the dead." This clearly reflects a very "high Christology" in which Jesus and God are equated. While this view gradually gained wide acceptance throughout the church, its bold expression here might suggest that 2 *Clement* was a relatively late text within our collection as opposed to the *Didache*, whose theology seems to reflect a very ancient view of the nature of Jesus as the Messiah.

The divine nature of the Christ is further endorsed in other writings, including the *Epistle to Diognetus*, whose author refers to Jesus as both the Child and Son of God. We find that it is to God's Son alone that the knowledge of the divine plan was given and the power to save the righteous was endowed. So too, Ignatius of Antioch speaks of the divine origins of the Christ in the various creeds that he offers, identifying the divine nature of Jesus through such phrases as "God in humanity . . . both of Mary and God," "the seed of David and the Holy Spirit," and "born of a virgin." So too, Polycarp refers to Jesus as the "Son of God" and as Savior of those who truly believe, depicting the Christ as God's divine agent in the world.

Such texts illustrate the diverse ways in which the authors of our collection viewed the nature of God. While it is clear that they had extended the strict nature of Jewish monotheism beyond its narrow boundaries, it is also certain that they were not in agreement with respect to what that meant for the ultimate details of a systematic Christian theology.

2. Ecclesiology (Church)

As with the matter of the nature of God, the second-century view of the character of the institutional church is widely varied among the Apostolic Fathers. Yet it is quite evident that our authors had generally advanced beyond Paul's own understanding of the issue. In his many New Testament letters, Paul clearly envisions the "body of Christ" to be the individual members of each faith community, participants who act in the world as the eyes, ears, and hands of Christian faith. In both a practical and mystical sense, Christians serve as the presence of Christ within the human race. Paul notes several types of people who guided this activity, including apostles, evangelists, teachers, and the elders whom he continually addresses in each letter. But these may be taken more as functions of the body of Christ than as strict offices. It is only with the later deuteroPauline letters of 1–2 Timothy and Titus that we find the roles of bishop, presbyter, and deacon defined as official posts of ecclesiastical leadership. Even the relatively late book of Acts only addresses the origins of the position of deacon, indicating no particular concern for the remaining two offices of church organization.

By the time of the Apostolic Fathers such offices had begun to take a more consistent shape and orientation. Even the *Didache*, which may be among the earliest of our writings, speaks of the need to appoint "bishops and deacons worthy of the Lord." Scholars have long debated whether the Didachist knew of the office of presbyter (perhaps included in the plural word "bishops") or, instead, represented a strain of early Christianity that knew of only two leadership positions. In either case, our author was clearly aware that the church had come to recognize the necessity of established roles of ecclesiastical leadership.

Perhaps the best-known perspective on hierarchy within the early church derives from the views of Ignatius of Antioch, whose three-tiered system ultimately came to dominate episcopal forms of Christianity in later centuries. In vibrant imagery that compares the offices of the church with the functions of divine authority, Ignatius argues for the legitimate roles of bishop, presbyter, and deacon. For him, deacons are seen as the presence of Jesus Christ in action within the church, presbyters represent the council of the apostles who serve God, and bishops embody the existence of God the Father within individual churches. The system of Ignatius is particularly concerned for the place of a single bishop over each church community, a man whom Ignatius perhaps envisions as the literal manifestation of God among Christians. No form of the Eucharist was considered to be valid without the authorization of the bishop. No matters of doctrinal debate were seen to be resolved without the bishop's approval.

While many modern Christians believe that the three-tiered system that Ignatius endorses was representative of the early second-century church in general, the situation may actually be quite the contrary. It is not at all certain that all churches followed a similar

75

pattern. The fact that Ignatius addresses the issue with such fervor within the letters that he writes along his journeys through Asia Minor actually suggests that he is forced to make a case for his views in many situations where Christians are perhaps following competing systems of authority. In a similar manner, the historian Eusebius of Caesarea often seems to be at great pains to recount the exact lineage of apostolic succession for important churches around the Mediterranean from his vantage point in the fourth century. Such endeavors suggest that Christians were not always in general agreement about the historical authority that lay behind the various doctrinal positions practiced among individual churches. In any case, the church is greatly indebted to Ignatius for the mono-episcopal hierarchy that now dominates church polity.

Considerations of early church development must necessarily extend beyond the question of hierarchy, of course. Instead, the broader issue of how the church envisioned itself and how it viewed its role within the wider world must be examined. And it is indeed here that the Apostolic Fathers offer some intriguing glimpses into how late first- and second-century Christians saw themselves as united practitioners of faith.

We begin once again with the *Didache*, whose instructional materials are primarily directed toward individual members of the church. The general tone of the *Didache* seems to suggest that the author is either writing very early in the development of the church's institutional consciousness or, instead, is working outside of the mainstream tradition. But at the same time, the various liturgical and ecclesiastical directions that are preserved in the text speak to the united nature of faith communities. The Didachist teaches that there are correct ways to baptize, to fast, to pray, to observe Eucharist, to observe the Lord's Day, and to select worthy leaders. It remains unclear whether our author intends these instructions to be directed toward a broad range of Christians who were scattered among numerous churches, or to the more restricted population of an individual congregation, or perhaps only to the leadership of a specific faith community. In either case, the *Didache* envisions a time when the church will be gathered together from its scattered places throughout the earth, brought into unity through the return of the Lord.

From the *Didache* we turn toward the tradition of Polycarp. In his single letter to the Philippians, Polycarp offers specific teachings with respect to the nature of being a Christian. It is clear that he holds righteousness to be the highest virtue of faith. First demanded by Jesus and then demonstrated by the apostle Paul, the bishop accepts the assertion that righteous Christians demonstrate a love that keeps them far from sin. Indeed, wives and husbands, children and widows, and deacons and presbyters can only fulfill their roles within the church to the extent that they are practitioners of righteousness. Polycarp makes this virtue the foundation upon which he preaches against the unrighteous desire for money and addresses the sins of the presbyter Valens, whose ignorance of his office has brought shame to his position within the church at Philippi.

The prominence that bishops like Polycarp and Ignatius bring to Christian life in the second-century is a clear indication that individual leaders were crucial in shaping the self-image of the institutional church. Ignatius undoubtedly was selected for arrest by Roman authorities in Antioch because he represented the broader church of the region as its primary figurehead. And the importance of Polycarp is clearly indicated in the fact that his final days have been preserved in the record of his martyrdom, written by members of his church in Smyrna and offered as an inspiration to faith for other congregations in Asia Minor.

Yet other images of the church must also be considered from our literature. One of the most influential of these descriptions appears in the *Shepherd*, whose author offers a portrayal of the church's development in two distinct ways. At the beginning of the work we find the church to be represented through the metaphorical image of a woman who addresses the hero, Hermas, on separate occasions. During the first encounter she is young and beautiful, but with subsequent appearances she has advanced into middle age and, finally, into a figure of full maturity. As his guide (the Shepherd) explains the situation to Hermas, the woman is the church, whose youth from the beginning of time was itself to evolve gradually into the more mature and glorious reality that God had envisioned.

The *Shepherd* eventually redirects this same vision of the church into a second image, the construction of a great tower. It is this figure that dominates the most sizable portion of the story's narrative, thus to indicate that the development of the church holds special importance for our author. The many virtues of Christian piety are active in the production of this church, a structure that is fixed upon a solid rock and features a special door through which only the righteous of God may pass. Angels are at work in this process, choosing as foundation stones the apostles, bishops, teachers, prophets, and deacons of the tradition, and laying upon them the worthy stones of those who are faithful and have suffered for God. This image of the church as a solid creation of divine guidance came to demand wide respect among later Christian theologians, particularly in the medieval period when the church had gained broad control throughout Europe.

Finally, we turn to the *Epistle to Diognetus*, whose author speaks of the church as an active presence within the world. Employing a semi-mystical understanding of the role of Christ throughout the human race, the author of *Diognetus* insists that Christians exist as foreigners among their fellow countrymen. They are citizens of the kingdom of God, living as resident aliens within a kingdom of earthly powers. Though they speak the same language and follow the same customs, Christians are to the world as the soul is to the body, present and yet separate. As individual members within the church, those who are faithful to Christ wait in a perishable world in anticipation of the coming of God's eternal kingdom. The image of Christians as the active presence of Christ in the world brings us full circle to the teachings of the apostle Paul. Though written over a century later, *Diognetus* has managed to recapture an essential component of how Paul saw the church as the body of Christ apart from a specific institutional consciousness. At the same time, later theologians eventually adapted the vision of Christians who belong to one kingdom but live in another in order to describe the nature of the church. This is most evident in Augustine's *City of God*, for example, which became a foundational text for many scholars who framed later views of the role of the church in society and culture.

3. Eschatology (Future)

There is considerable debate among biblical scholars about the degree to which Jesus of Nazareth was concerned for the end of time in his teachings. And yet, there is near unanimous agreement that the early church was extremely interested in the topic. In Paul's first letter to the Thessalonians, the oldest correspondence that we have from his hand and the earliest complete piece of literature in the New Testament, a major driving force behind the apostle's theology is the need to remain watchful as Christians await the return of the Lord. While some would insist that this was a peculiar tendency of Paul's own theology, it seems much more likely that his views reflected the wide-ranging concerns of the early church.

The Gospel of Mark offers similar teachings from the lips of Jesus that are grouped into a unified discourse in chapter 13. Both the Gospels of Matthew and Luke, having made use of Mark's Gospel, expanded this material by adding additional teachings. The author of Matthew continued even further by interlacing the entire Matthean text with apocalyptic warnings and comments that refer specifically to the end of time. Beyond the gospels, one need only look to 2 Peter and Jude for additional evidence of early church concern for the end times. And, of course, Christian history has always acknowledged the eschatological nature of the book of Revelation.

It is through Revelation, in fact, that we perhaps best come to understand the role of eschatology and apocalyptic literature in the Apostolic Fathers. Indeed, those early Christian leaders who compiled the New Testament placed Revelation at the conclusion of the canon for two reasons. Most obviously, it spoke of last things and thus should appear in the final literary position. But too, it offered an urgency that those who believe in Christ should turn from their sinful ways immediately. In other words, threats about the end of time and a final, future judgment were often employed to emphasize the need for Christians to repent, set straight their values, and live as serious believers in Christ. The same tendency holds true to this day.

The author of the *Didache* treats apocalyptic literature in the same way as the patristic theologians who framed the New Testament canon, by placing such concerns at the end of the literary corpus. For the most part the text of the *Didache* makes little reference to the last times, offering only scattered, oblique allusions throughout various liturgical materials in phrases like "your kingdom come" and "may your church be gathered together from the ends of the earth," as well as in the code word "Maranatha" (Our Lord come!). Otherwise, the Didachist saves all of the work's apocalyptic materials for the concluding section of the work, chapter 16. It is here that the reader is warned to "be alert" for the coming of the Lord. In the days of false prophets and corrupters the deceiver of the world will appear on the earth. But God will bring a fiery test for humanity, and then the Lord shall come on the clouds with the sound of a trumpet. While this language may actually reflect the concerns of the Didachist for what may happen in the future, it seems much more likely that such imagery is calculated to motivate the readers of the *Didache* to pay attention to the many teachings that occupy the preceding fifteen chapters.

Elsewhere in the Apostolic Fathers there are several authors who have made a much more concerted effort to write apocalyptic imagery and eschatological themes into their principal narrative. We need only turn to the *Epistle of Barnabas* to see these elements at work. The author of *Barnabas* clearly endorses a very dualistic view of the world, envisioning the reality of evil at work in the present corrupt generation and hoping for the future dawn of God's justice in the last days. *Barnabas* makes use of Isaiah 40 in exploiting this vision, noting the observation that "the Lord and his reward are at hand." The author's close association with Jewish texts and traditions continues along this same stream of thought. Writing from a millenarian view that was typical of many early Christians from the late-first and early-second centuries, *Barnabas* makes use of the six days of creation that are recalled in the opening verses of Genesis as a framework for interpreting the close of history. These "days" are not to be taken literally. Instead, they represent a period of six thousand years after which the Lord will return to punish those who have forsaken God's covenant and to reward the repentant souls who believe in Christ. Elements from the book of Daniel are interwoven into this interpretation of the end of time, mainly our author's views of contemporary history in the light of the ten kingdoms about which the prophet had warned.

From the arguments of *Barnabas* we may turn to the perspective of Ignatius, whose letters throughout Asia Minor offer reflections of his concern for the end of time. Some scholars have observed that Ignatius does not hold any particular perspective that is worthy of note in this regard, since the bishop is quite naturally more concerned for his anticipated death in Rome. But various clues survive within his letters. For example, he recalls for the church in Ephesus that these are indeed the last times, a period to remain strong and persistent in Christian faith. And he offers his hope that at the future resurrection he will be counted as worthy together with those who constitute the Ephesian church. In his letter to the church at Philadelphia he observes that there is a kingdom of God that is yet to be inherited. And to the Trallians he writes that God the Father will raise up all those who believe in Christ Jesus. To the Magnesians he notes that everything has its end and that all people must eventually take their place in eternity.

In many ways Ignatius envisions that the future kingdom of God has already encroached upon the present. While the forces of evil focus their energy to bring the bishop to a disreputable end through the agency of Rome, he feels that his death will be a worthy testimony to his faith in Christ. He preaches to the members of the church in Rome that he actually wants to be a "martyr" (witness) in their presence. For it is through just such an end, torn by savage beasts and tortured beyond endurance, that he hopes to prove his full and faithful discipleship to God's will. Scholars have observed that this language may be more than metaphorical imagery for Ignatius. To some extent it is easy to imagine that he quite literally saw his death as the denouement to a divine plan that he was completing for God on behalf of the church.

Finally, we turn quickly to two works, the *Shepherd of Hermas* and *2 Clement*. With respect to the *Shepherd*, it is clear that a concern for the end times is paramount for our author's theology. Unfortunately, the nature of that vision remains ambiguous. Phrases such as "the last day" and "great tribulation to come" are to be discovered everywhere throughout the text. The promise of the coming master and the future day in which the church will find its completion in God's kingdom are crucial to our author's view of history and to God's role within it. At the same time, however, there is much talk about the present church and the need for the Spirit of God to provide some direction for Christians, offering leadership for immediate needs and future crises. And while Hermas along his way encounters a great beast (the Leviathan), very reflective of a similar beast in the book of Revelation, this creature permits him to pass in a docile manner with God's help. No great battle occurs. The future has not yet arrived.

In *2 Clement*, there is a continuing emphasis upon eschatology. Christ is judge of the living and dead and will reward the faithful in future days. Only repentance and a pure lifestyle can bring Christians to the salvation that God alone offers The final section of the work, chapters 15–20, is consumed with the conviction that God's judgment is at hand. The need for prayer is emphasized for each reader, and the importance of turning to the commands of the Lord is affirmed. It is true that there will be great suffering for those who remain faithful to God in the present world. But the ultimate rewards that Christ offers are worthy of the effort.

4. Orthodoxy (Unity)

Perhaps the greatest challenge in the early church was the peril of division and separation both between and within the many communities of faith that arose around the Mediterranean world. The conviction of early Christians was great. Their dedication to a new life in Christ and to an existence that respected both God and neighbor is evident in the many writings they have left for our consideration. At the same time, however, the specific details of how that life was to be lived often became the focus of great debate. In some respects, quarrels arose over the need to remain faithful to Jewish cultic and liturgical practices; in other ways, clashes developed over the necessity to bring outsiders into the community who were unaware of Jewish customs and were insensitive to the issues that those traditions attempted to protect. But further, the various subtle facets of early Christian theology demanded a careful consideration of many details of faith and conviction that rarely gained a broad consensus among churches and often led to broad divisions of perspective. The resulting debates are well documented in the New Testament. We recall that Paul confronted the Corinthians about their strange behavior toward one another. And the author of 1 John decried the heretical teachings of those who had come forth from his own church but who clearly were not in agreement with its wisdom.

The Apostolic Fathers also recognize the threat of division. And their many authors are generally concerned to avoid disagreements and to bond all Christians into a unified believing body of Christ. It is perhaps this single theme that is most commonly shared among our texts, the need for consensus of opinion and unity of perspective among the churches. From the author of *1 Clement* in Rome to the writings of Ignatius from Antioch, from the Didachist in the eastern Mediterranean to the author of the *Shepherd* in Italy, the quest for Christian unity in practice and theology stood as a primary foundation upon which the early church sought to erect its walls.

The easiest place to begin an examination of the idea of orthodoxy within the Apostolic Fathers is with Ignatius. His letters are replete with charges against two specific groups: those who wanted to return the church to its Jewish moorings (= Judaizers) and those who denied that Christ had actually come in human form but rather in spirit only (= Docetists). Both debates were rampant among early Christians, with roots that are easily traced to biblical authors.

Ignatius himself was certainly dependent upon the writings of Paul for his arguments against the pro-Jewish tendency among certain Christians, especially as portrayed within Paul's letter to the Galatians. As we have discussed above, Ignatius had no particular sympathy for Jewish traditions and rituals. He was primarily concerned for Christianity's movement away from its Palestinian roots. As some scholars have argued, the bishop's vision of a threefold hierarchy of leadership may have been based upon a Hellenistic model that was employed in numerous social guilds that were widely recognized throughout the Roman Empire. In either case, he had no great desire to return to a theologically conservative view of Jewish Christianity that he himself had never experienced.

With respect to the threat of Docetism, 1–3 John and the book of Revelation already indicate the degree to which such ideas were popular throughout Asia Minor. The approach of Ignatius to the problem appears to have been somewhat unique for his time, employing creeds as a standard by which orthodox faith could be assured in disputes of doctrine. As he states in his letter to the Ephesians, "there is one physician, both flesh and spirit, born and unborn, God in humanity," and to the Trallians, "Jesus Christ was from the line of David, of Mary, was truly born, both ate and drank, was truly persecuted."[6] With such clearly stated creeds he could assure that his readership was in agreement with his view that those who believed that Christ had come in spirit alone were simply wrong. It was to just such creeds that the later church made great appeal in establishing the parameters of what was to be recognized as orthodox faith about the nature of Jesus as the Messiah and the significance of his life and death for human salvation.

For Ignatius it is necessary that all Christians who are united in the one, true "catholic" (universal) church should be in agreement with respect to matters of theology and faith. There is no room for division or for the false doctrines that Ignatius labels as "strange food" and "evil teaching." Unity is of paramount concern. And for Ignatius, that unity is only available under the presence of a bishop.

Other writers within our corpus undoubtedly are in agreement with this general emphasis of Ignatius. The bishop Polycarp, for example, offers advice that clearly reflects the Ignatian horror of Docetic challenges to sound doctrine: "everyone who does not confess that Jesus Christ came in the flesh is an antichrist!"[7] And as Polycarp observes further, those who twist the teachings of Jesus to suit their own evil desires are the firstborn of Satan. This teaching could hardly be more definitively stated. It clearly places Polycarp within the same theological stream as Ignatius. In a similar vein, the Didachist warns against persons who lead Christians away from the way of the teaching that the *Didache* endorses. Those prophets who teach the truth but do not follow that teaching in their own practice are also to be shunned. Of particular concern are those persons that the Didachist calls "Christ merchants," individuals who only appear to be faithful followers of Christian belief, but who actually peddle the gospel message for their own material gain. It seems that early in the rise of the Christian enterprise the church was already involved in a process by which pseudo-Christians had to be identified and separated from true believers.

The author of *1 Clement* offers additional insight into the nature of Christian unity. Based upon the Old Testament imagery of God's divine guidance of ancient Israel through the selected leadership of Moses, our author encourages the church to submit to a similar process by which the apostolic tradition of Christ might provide direction to individual churches as they evolve through history. In this process, the best avenue by which to envision a unified community of faith is to follow the model of teacher and prophet that Jesus of Nazareth provided. The authority of Christ as God's divine agent is demonstrated in the orderliness of sound community leadership. On the one hand, organized churches are sound communities of faith. On the other hand, congregations that experience factionalism and theological tension are weak in their devotion to God. In the same way that God created the world with order and precision to follow a set path of functions, so too did God intend the church to fulfill a preconceived plan of gospel faith and moral living that was worthy of its charter.

Finally, we turn once more to the *Shepherd*. The author of this writing appears to be less concerned for the unity of the church with respect to theological issues and more interested in a unified household of faith as demonstrated by the correct ethical lifestyle of its individual members. An intriguing element of the *Shepherd* is the recognition that the presence of God's Holy Spirit within the community of faith actually brings order and structure to the church, not division and conflict. The many images of the text may be directly applied to this conclusion. Rich and poor Christians are like strong trees and vines, the one to offer support and the other to provide comfort. All of the community's faithful followers are to work in the vineyard of God's kingdom, serving the church together. And all types of Christians are to live as one without prejudice until that time when the Eternal Judge will separate the wheat from the chaff. As the *Shepherd* notes, it is through the virtuous traits of simplicity, innocence, purity, patience, fear of the Lord, cheerfulness, and patience in suffering that the church honors God. These qualities provide unity for the church. And those Christians who observe them on a daily basis are able to turn away false prophecy and evil desires. Indeed, unity is the key for righteous living.

5. Soteriology (Salvation)

At the core of early Christian concerns about the faith of the church was the nagging question of how humanity could be saved. This question was typically offered against the background of divergent views of the world. According to some perspectives, the cosmos was created by God as a beautiful home for humanity that people themselves had corrupted by turning away from the divine intention for their lives. In the view of other theologians, the world could be divided into two opposing spheres of influence, the first sphere being dominated by the power of evil and opposed to the will of God, and the second being ruled as the divine kingdom of God's influence and power. These cosmological views often came into conflict whenever Christians discussed the nature of the world and the role of human faith in daily living. But rarely did early Christian authors dispute the necessity of all humanity to turn from an impulse for sin and toward the salvation that God offers through the Son of Man.

The author of *1 Clement* provides a perspective of this situation that is strikingly parallel to various New Testament texts and that helped the patristic church to develop a systematic way of thinking about the nature of salvation. According to our author, the blood of Jesus was poured out for the salvation of humanity and provided the grace of repentance to the whole world. This focus upon the blood of Christ is a truly significant motif throughout *1 Clement*. Our author observes that the color of blood was anticipated in the scarlet thread that Rahab used to save the spies of Israel in Jericho. And the blood of martyrs reflects the ultimate sacrifice that the Son of God made upon the cross for the salvation of all people who believe in his name. To a large extent this focus upon blood and sacrifice, caught up in the image of the Lord Jesus Christ as the "High Priest" of God, reflects a motif that appears in the book of Hebrews. The concern of both authors is clearly Jewish in orientation, particularly as it relates to the need for some sort of priestly sacrifice to God the Father on behalf of a sinful people. And in this respect the primary theme of *1 Clement*, that is, the need for order and divine guidance, finds a home in the author's concern for the church's salvation through Christ.

The theme of salvation through the blood of Christ is also found in the writings of Ignatius and Polycarp. The various creeds that Ignatius offers are largely oriented toward the suffering of the Messiah. For Ignatius, the theological conviction that Jesus of Nazareth had been truly persecuted, crucified, and killed as a historical moment under the rule of Pontius Pilate was a necessity for human salvation. Only under these particular circumstances could Christians then offer the claim that Jesus Christ had been raised from the dead by God the Father as the first fruit of those who hoped to be resurrected in his name. One can easily see the dangerous threat that Docetism offered to this theme of salvation. For if the Messiah had not actually come in human flesh, then he could not have suffered death in the same way as those who followed him. His own fate would not have been tied to that of his disciples. This theme within early Christianity came to serve as a foundational pillar for later theology, standing as a linchpin for further speculation about the nature of resurrection and afterlife in God's eternal kingdom.

Another aspect of salvation through the blood of Christ is seen in the issue of martyrdom. This theme was a key motivation behind the writings of Ignatius, who anticipated that his own death in Rome would serve as a blood-sacrifice witness of his faith in Christ. Yet the best view of this motif within early Christianity is found in the death of Polycarp as preserved in the *Martyrdom of Polycarp*. As discussed above, the author of this work carefully portrays the details of Polycarp's arrest, interrogation, and execution against parallel narrative elements of the passion of Jesus of Nazareth from the New Testament Gospels. But what is most important in this depiction is the general tone that dominates the recollection of the bishop's death. His sacrifice of faith is clearly not undertaken for personal glory in the eyes of God, but as a worthy disciple's imitation of his master. It is certainly true that the death of Polycarp is viewed as evidence of the bishop's righteousness as a follower of Christ. At the same time, the reader gets the distinct impression that other faithful Christians can find their own salvation in imitation of Polycarp's sacrifice. It is often observed that the framework of the *Martyrdom* soon came to dominate the presentation of later martyrologies, the recollection of subsequent Christians who were arrested and persecuted by civil authorities. The death of Polycarp seems to have become a template upon which the depiction of other Christian deaths were structured. In any event, it is clear that the literary witnesses to Ignatius' anticipated death in Christ and Polycarp's own martyrdom were quickly seen by the church as a lens through which to envision the depth of faith that Christian martyrs held for their beliefs.

Yet another text that should be considered here is the *Epistle of Barnabas*. While our author is largely concerned that each reader should pay particular attention to a triptych of key Christian virtues (faith, righteousness, joy), the role of the Messiah's death is central to an understanding of these elements. As the author explains, the covenant of salvation that God offered to Israel has been transferred to anyone who will accept that the crucifixion of the Lord was for the forgiveness of sins. Moses and the prophets attested to this graciousness of God, and the Old Testament offered images of its reality in the sacrifice of the red heifer, the scapegoat ritual, the symbols of water and the cross, and the spiritual restoration of the Temple within the lives of all Christians. The essential conviction of *Barnabas* is that the sacrifice of the Lord Jesus Christ upon the cross was on behalf of all people of faith. And the reality of that act underlies the belief that salvation is available to anyone who will follow God's commands.

Of course, not all the writings of the Apostolic Fathers are necessarily focused upon the imagery of blood and sacrificial death as a primary axis of human salvation. The text of the *Didache*, for example, seems to be largely focused upon the necessity of living a philosophy that the author calls "the way of life," an approach to Christian existence that *Barnabas* 18–20 labels "the way of light" and that is paralleled to some extent within the views of *2 Clement*. The core conviction of these writings is that Christians must seek to follow a certain path of righteous living, as opposed to a path of evil and destruction, in order to assure their salvation in the kingdom of God. On the one hand, this will lead to a successful life in the present world; on the other, it will assure rewards in the world to come. This orientation toward righteous living was not original to early Christianity, whose followers found it already at work in the book of Deuteronomy and in ancient Israel's wisdom literature. Parallel beliefs are even evident in the writings of the Dead Sea Scrolls. Yet it is intriguing that many early Christians came to focus upon their own contemporary life of faith as a primary way in which they could adequately respond to the will of God, with little specific concern for the salvific role of the death of Jesus.

To some extent the witness of the *Didache* suggests that the focus upon the cross of Christ that was preached by the apostle Paul, preserved in the passion narratives of the Gospels, and certified by authors within the Apostolic Fathers was not the only way in which Christians of the late first century understood the role of Jesus of Nazareth for their salvation. In addition to this central premise that has become a key to the theology of mainline Christianity, the *Didache* provides a powerful argument for following specific teachings of the faith tradition as the central foundation for living in Christ. Ultimately the patristic church incorporated this sage wisdom as an important subset of its own particular confession about salvation through the cross.

CHAPTER 5

Structures of the Ancient Church

As most people would assume, the Apostolic Fathers represent a period in early Christian history that spanned the
gap between the writings of the New Testament and the
more mature reflections of later theologians such as Irenaeus,
Origen, Athanasius, and Augustine. In many respects our collected works form a conduit between the earliest faith confessions of
Christianity and the better developed formation of the institutional church that evolved into today's mainline traditions.

At the same time, however, those persons who authored the
writings that now form the Apostolic Fathers have preserved a
variety of theological insights and institutional considerations that
do not show any obvious dependence upon scripture. It is difficult
to know the extent to which such ideas generally circulated within
the broad conversations of early Christians. Often we must
assume that they simply represent the speculation of an individual author or the community of faith in which a particular text
was written. In either case, our collected works offer a broad variety of opinions that were eventually to gain popularity among
patristic authors, sometimes triggering further conversations that
came to have significant impact upon the evolution of ecclesiastical thought and doctrine. Though one might easily devote an
entire volume to this topic, it will be sufficient for our present pur-

poses to survey briefly some of the more intriguing and important of these ideas here.

We have already alluded to our first topic for consideration, that is, the nature of early Christian ministry. The Apostolic Fathers are certainly not united on this issue. As previously noted, Ignatius of Antioch endorses a specific approach within each faith community that features a single bishop, a college of presbyters, and a division of deacons. As noted above, many modern Christians assume that this Ignatian system actually reflects a scheme of church administration that was commonly practiced throughout the Mediterranean world by the end of the first century. But in fact, it is much more likely that it was Ignatius himself who made the structure popular by the emphasis that he gives to it throughout his letters.

When one surveys biblical literature, there are few places where the views of Ignatius are so clearly indicated. The book of Acts mentions the ordination of deacons, but no bishops or presbyters. And while Paul typically addressed his correspondence to "elders" (the same word as presbyters), his audience may have simply envisioned their ecclesiastical duties in reference to the position of synagogue elders and not as part of a larger hierarchy of authority. It is only in the Pastoral Epistles that we find the ranks of bishops, deacons, and presbyters addressed together, though even here their relationship is not explained. Within this literature there are also a variety of other offices listed and described that Ignatius does not bother to incorporate into his power structure, including the roles of apostles, prophets, teachers, and widows.

Other writings within the Apostolic Fathers bring a problematic air to the system that Ignatius endorses. The *Didache*, for example, speaks of bishops and deacons together without presbyters. This may suggest that the community of the Didachist was unaware of the role of presbyter, though some scholars insist that our author envisions bishops and presbyters together as the same office or, instead, that the text actually assumes presbyters to be the audience. At the same time, the author of *1 Clement* also speaks only of bishops and deacons, based upon a misreading of the Greek translation of Isaiah 60:17: "I will appoint their bishops in righteousness and their deacons in faith." Despite the claims of common ecclesiastical tradition, there is no clear indication that a single bishop originally guided the church at Rome, the community in which *1 Clement* was written. Neither Paul nor Ignatius addresses his letter for Rome to any particular leader within the community. And the text of *1 Clement* makes no particular claim to episcopal authority in its efforts to help the Corinthian church to resolve its struggles with power and influence. Indeed, the roots of Roman church governance remain murky.

In addition to bishops and deacons, both the *Didache* and *1 Clement* mention the role of apostles and prophets. There were two types of apostles: those recognized as members of "the Twelve" who traveled with Jesus of Nazareth and carried his approval to preach in his name, and those who like Paul and Barnabas were authorized by the Jerusalem church to journey to specific faith communities in order to preach and teach the Christian gospel message. Both positions were ultimately destined to disappear of course. The first type of apostle vanished as its membership reached the end of their lives; the second type ceased to exist with the fundamental destruction of the Jerusalem church during the Jewish War of 66–73 C.E.

The role of prophet is perhaps even more interesting than that of apostle with respect to the development of ecclesiastical hierarchy. It is clear both from the New Testament and from the Apostolic Fathers that Christian prophets circulated far and wide throughout the Roman Empire. Paul calls himself a prophet and acts as a visionary spokesperson for Christ. The authors of 2 Peter, 1–3 John, Revelation, and the Gospels warn against false prophets whose teachings confused the beliefs of Christ's followers. The Didachist and Ignatius also warn against false prophets, many of whom were sham Christians who had come to identify the financial benefit that "preaching Christ" could bring to their personal wealth.

It is clear that there were two types of prophets in ancient Christianity, those who traveled randomly between churches and those who maintained some permanent position within a single faith community. It was the former group that led to much early consternation, since there was a hesitancy to accept the strange teachings of outsiders, on the one hand, and a reluctance to be proven wrong when accusing them of false practices, on the other. The latter group, local prophets, often had a dominant role in the daily life and worship of individual churches. But with the firm

93

establishment of administrators like bishops, deacons, and presbyters, their influence waned in due course. And the position of
prophet within the hierarchy of the church disappeared. Indeed,
true Christian prophets eventually sought to live and work at the
fringes of ecclesiastical control. Many came to assume the solitary
and spiritual lives of hermits, while others organized monasteries
that sustained similar faith values among their members.
Ultimately, the association of the Holy Spirit with prophecy, combined with a strong suspicion of the role of the Spirit among dubi-
ous ecstatic movements of the second century, eventually led to a
fading of the role of Christian prophets within the structure of the
patristic church.

Of particular interest in any discussion of early church leadership is the development of distinctions between clergy and laity
that evolved during the period of our writings. The apostle Paul
spoke of certain religious leadership functions such as apostle,
teacher, and evangelist, but never suggested that there should be a
fundamental difference between the value of clergy and laity
within the church. For him, all members of the body of Christ
have an important role in whatever capacity they might fill. By the
time of the Apostolic Fathers, however, it is clear that leaders
within individual church communities have a responsibility for
integrity and leadership that sets them apart from the common
role of other Christians. Both Ignatius and Polycarp make this
clear in their letters. And the author of *1 Clement* stresses the
importance of ecclesiastical hierarchy in the maintenance of the
apostolic tradition, without which no individual church may lay
claim to a legitimate role in the kingdom of God. We must simply
assume that any argument for the significance of the clergy necessarily implies a demotion for the role of the laity.

At the same time, there are other texts within our collection that
do not suggest that there is any essential difference in the importance of clergy versus laity. The *Didache*, for example, appears to
offer the way of life to all believers and emphasizes that the
responsibility for maintaining true faith in Christian teaching and
tradition should be placed at the door of all who would follow the
Lord. It is true that the Didachist mentions specific ecclesiastical
offices such as apostle, prophet, bishop, and deacon, but there is
no particular indication that their crucial spiritual and liturgical

functions make them any more important than other Christians within the faith community.

By the same token, the *Shepherd of Hermas, 2 Clement,* and the *Epistle to Diognetus* provide no special claim for the role of clergy. What God has done for human salvation through the cross of Christ and through the power of the Holy Spirit is meant for all Christians and may be seen within the work in which each church member is engaged. Each of these authors holds individual Christians to be responsible for their own lives of faith, with no special accountability to a special class of clerical leaders. But of course, one must admit that it is difficult to know what the assumptions of our authors really are with respect to clergy-laity distinctions. Silence on a subject does not always lead to good insights.

This brings us to the matter of how clerical functions developed within the institutional church. Scholars have broadly debated this issue for many years. The New Testament offers little instruction with respect to liturgical and pastoral roles for Christian priests. It is true that we see the metaphorical image of Christ at work as High Priest in the book of Hebrews. And here we find a seminal image of Christ at work as mediator between divinity and humanity, serving both as the priest who offers sacrifice to God and as the sacrifice itself. The author of Hebrews taps into the slippery tradition of Melchizedek from Genesis for this image, making use of a mystical figure from antiquity that became the subject of considerable debate among early Christians and Gnostics alike. But such visions can only offer a limited perspective upon what the role of the Christian ministerial priesthood was ultimately to become. In reality, the eventual functions of priests within the ecclesiastical tradition were finally patterned upon the parallel roles of Jewish priests, whose work at the Temple and whose duties in the synagogues were based upon Old Testament notions. The responsibility of mediation between God and humanity, the call to lead the faithful in prayer and worship, the right to claim special privilege with respect to tithes and offerings, and the task of serving as pastor and guide for all Christians were all derived from Old Testament foundations, roots that provided a framework for Jewish priests and rabbis as well.

Much like their Jewish counterparts, early Christian leaders soon became the directors of ritual and liturgy within religious settings. It is quite likely that the bulk of the church's liturgical practices were based upon Jewish roots that can be traced to first-century synagogues. For example, the singing of hymns and the offering of prayers that employed the Old Testament Psalms were typical of ancient Christian worship as it was observed in various house churches around the Mediterranean. So too, the development of homilies as a motivation to faith and an assurance for Christians in the midst of cultural and religious struggle clearly reflects rabbinic practices during the first century.

The early church's dependence upon Jewish traditions and insights is well documented throughout the New Testament. The Gospels, for example, have made considerable use of Old Testament texts and motifs to provide a comprehensive picture of who Jesus of Nazareth was as the Son of God. Most important within this process was a variety of prophetic texts that were drawn from materials in the Psalms, Isaiah, Jeremiah, Ezekiel and the so-called Minor Prophets of the Hebrew Bible. At the same time, the books of the Pentateuch, 1–2 Samuel, and 1–2 Kings are widely employed to demonstrate how Jesus was the fulfillment of depictions of the "prophet like Moses" that many Jews had anticipated from their reading of scripture. This same imagery was applied to the compilation of very specific collections of Christian writings, such as the Sermon on the Mount, which were intended to be symbolic presentations of Jesus in the role of Moses as the recipient of God's Torah on Mount Sinai. It is also applied to very specific liturgical moments, such as the presentation of the bread and wine by Jesus during the Passover meal, a historical moment that initiated the ritual of Eucharist that Christians soon came to recognize as a sacrament.

Because of the broad background of Jewish traditions behind numerous early Christian rituals, at least from among those that are known from the New Testament, it is perhaps all the more interesting that so few of these same materials are preserved in our Apostolic Fathers. Indeed, most of our authors indicate no particular concern to discuss the specifics of early Christian liturgy in their works. We might speculate that the Jewish heritage of ecclesiastical liturgy was so broadly recognized among Christians that there was no particular need to address it in literary discussions. At the same time, it does not seem that the writings in our

Apostolic Fathers necessarily were directed toward that particular task, having instead been constructed to address issues of faith, ethical lifestyle, hierarchy, and the authority of Christ.

But this is not to suggest that the Apostolic Fathers say nothing about Christian liturgy and worship. The *Shepherd of Hermas,* for example, comments upon two important aspects of this matter. The first of these is the significance of prayer as a crucial link between Christ's faithful followers and the divine guidance that comes from God. As our author observes, it is impossible to follow the commandments of God without the daily assistance of the Holy Spirit, the presence of God that gladly lives in a clean house of faith and provides the means by which Christians may persevere through evil times. Our author truly recognizes the value of the Spirit both in the liturgical context and in the daily life of Christians.

The second facet is related to the question of human weakness, particularly as it is witnessed after baptism. With special focus upon the issues of adultery, divorce, and remarriage, the *Shepherd* is fully aware that, though Christian baptism is intended to wash away sins and assure salvation, the human nature of Christians eventually leads them into sinful actions once more. How then is forgiveness for such sins to be found? As our author observes, anyone who sins must be received if they repent, but not repeatedly, "for there is only one repentance for God's servants."[1] This early effort of our author to address the problem of sin in the ancient church, specifically on the occasion of broken marriages, ultimately evolved into the modern sacrament of penance, a rite whose broad application is intended to provide full restitution in the eyes of God and the church for any Christian whose baptism has been soiled by the weakness of human nature. And this must hold true for any believer who sins. Indeed, while the liturgical calendar of Judaism provides an opportunity for the corporate forgiveness of sin through its annual Day of Atonement ritual, Christian tradition renders such efforts to be the personal responsibility of believers through the avenue of individual penance.

The bishop Ignatius addresses two other liturgical rituals as foundational elements of the Christian life. The first of these is baptism, a concept that Ignatius assumes to be fundamental to the liturgical life of the church. Much like the apostle Paul, Ignatius understands the disposition of a Christian to be the avenue through which a believer may participate in the body of Christ both physically and spiritually. And it is to this goal of union with Christ that Christians must aspire, since the body of Christ is seen to be both pure and flawless. The question that arose within the early church, naturally, was that of why Jesus of Nazareth himself consented to be baptized, since tradition assumed that he already was without sin. On a historical level there is little doubt that the baptism of Jesus actually occurred, since its recollection by the church was something of an embarrassment for early Christian theology. Otherwise, one might presume that the Gospels would have omitted the scene from their accounts in order to avoid any inconvenient explanation of why a "sinless" savior needed baptism. But its presence in all four New Testament Gospels suggests, instead, that it was widely known among Christians. It is Ignatius who responds to this liturgical confusion in a most unique way. For in writing to the Ephesians about the heritage of Jesus, being both the seed of David and the Holy Spirit, he notes: "He was born and was baptized in order that through his suffering he might purify the water."[2] In other words, the water of Christian baptism only holds the properties of salvation for the church because Christ himself first purified it through his own act of baptism. This interpretation of why Jesus permitted himself to be baptized was not widely adopted by later patristic theologians and may only represent the thoughts of Ignatius. But it offers an intriguing glimpse into the bishop's speculation about the theological meaning behind a particular sacramental act.

The other sacrament upon which Ignatius comments is that of the Eucharist. He makes quite specific observations about this rite on numerous occasions, employing words that had serious ramifications for later liturgical beliefs. Most importantly, as noted above, he insists that no Eucharist is valid without the direction of a local bishop or his personal agent. In this way one can see the division that was established between bishops within the approved apostolic tradition and those disapproved leaders of competing Christian sects who were not in harmony with the so-called "catholic" church. Ultimately, Ignatius provides a framework upon which the ancient church was able to establish its validity as a singular institution under the guidance of Christ in contrast to "heretical" communities that did not share either the orthodox theology of the apostolic tradition or its liturgical rites. In addition, Ignatius believes that the bread of the Eucharist must be seen as the actual flesh of Jesus and not simply as a symbolic token of the reality of Christ. To confess that the bread is actual flesh requires a Christian to also acknowledge that Jesus Christ has himself actually come in the flesh, and not just as some phantasm in a spiritual body. The result is that Ignatius can employ the elements of the Eucharist as a theological counter to the trend of Docetism that had arisen within the church, especially in the eastern Mediterranean world. Thus, a common sacrament could become a weapon in a major theological controversy. The idea of "real body and real blood" ultimately became the foundation of the church's later understanding of the dogma of transubstantiation, the belief that Christ is truly present in the substance of the bread and wine at the Eucharist.

Any discussion of liturgical materials within the Apostolic Fathers must ultimately lead to the intriguing text of the *Didache*, whose author has preserved several elements of early Christian worship. These materials stand at the very center of the text and are associated with baptism, fasting, prayer, and Eucharist (chapters 7–10). In each instance we detect a concern for Jewish traditions and rituals, but these are typically cast within the light of specific Christian considerations. For example, the reader is instructed that baptism is to be conducted in "living" (running) water that is cold. This process would reflect the typical rabbinic requirements for purification rituals that were practiced by Jews in the first and second centuries. At the same time, however, the Didachist offers the caveat that if cold running water is not available, then warm standing water is acceptable. In each case, however, baptism must be accompanied by the Trinitarian blessing of the Father, Son, and Holy Spirit.

In brief comments upon fasting and prayer the Didachist simply assumes that Christians, like Jews, are participants in both activities. And yet, the reader is told that fasts and prayers are not to be observed like the "hypocrites" (presumably the Jews). Instead, fasts should be observed on Wednesdays and Fridays (versus the Jewish preference for Mondays and Thursdays). And prayer should be offered to God three times each day according to the model of the Lord's Prayer that has been preserved elsewhere in Matthew 6. This is all that the Didachist offers on these two topics. It is clear that with these brief observations the issue is considered to be closed. One might argue that the most crucial aspect of what the *Didache* has to offer here is a redirection of Christian liturgical practices away from their Jewish heritage. Yet, at the same time, there seems to be some truth in the recognition that the Didachist is less concerned about Judaism's heritage and more disturbed by the unsatisfactory way in which contemporary Jews employed their rituals and traditions to exclude the remaining nations of the world. But the issue remains unresolved.

Finally, the Didachist gives quite specific directions with respect to how the reader is to offer "thanksgiving" to God during the course of a meal. The Greek word for "to give thanks" is the same term that is typically translated into English by the word Eucharist. But in the case of the *Didache* this presents a certain problem for Christian theologians. Specifically, the Didachist offers only a series of prayers here and does not include any of the words of institution about the nature of the bread and cup, words that are preserved elsewhere in the Gospels. The prayers of the *Didache* are generally recognized as reworded versions of traditional Jewish blessings that were to be spoken over meals. Thus they reflect the influence of Jewish tradition and ritual. The inclusion of phrases like "Jesus, your servant," "may your church be gathered," and "remember your church" indicates that they have been specifically oriented toward Christian concerns. But there is no explicit reference to the words that modern Christians use during Eucharist.

In order to address this intriguing situation, scholars have offered a variety of solutions. Some have argued that the liturgical event to which the Didachist alludes here is not actually a Eucharist at all, but a "love feast." Speculation about the historical reality of such a ritual among ancient Christians has been extensive, but if it ever actually occurred, this text in the *Didache* would be our only remaining textual evidence for the ritual. Other scholars have suggested that our text preserves an unusual form of the Eucharist that was observed by a singular church community whose "backwater" isolation kept it separated from the evolution of mainline liturgical tradition. In other words, the community of

the *Didache* simply did not know or perhaps chose to reject the traditional celebration of the Eucharist that is common in the church
today. But a third solution to the situation may be found in the
possibility that the Eucharistic ritual that the Didachist has preserved represents a variation of our mainline practice that was
highly influenced by Jewish rituals and blessings. In fact, what
may be offered to us here is a unique glimpse into an isolated
church's celebration of the Eucharist that was dependent both
upon the commonly employed words of institution, which are not
preserved by the Didachist but are simply assumed, and time-
honored Jewish prayers that were eventually omitted from the literary tradition during the evolution of the ritual. It is difficult to
know which, if any, of these solutions may be correctly applied to
the situation of the *Didache* and the form of the Eucharist that it
preserves. But in either case, it is clear that our text contains an
interesting witness to the structures of the early church as it
sought to develop its own liturgical practices.

There are a variety of other ways in which the church of the second century struggled to develop its self-identity. A number of
these features are preserved in the Apostolic Fathers as unique
aspects of what it meant to be a Christian in the early patristic
period.

Perhaps the most obvious way in which early Christians sought
to establish their identity among the religious cultures of the
Mediterranean was through the establishment of very specific
approaches to a lifestyle of morality and ethics. This is a theme
that tends to come through in nearly all of the works in our collection, sometimes as a surface reflection of contemporary
Christianity and sometimes as the primary element of a particular
writing. The consideration of ethics within the evolution of the
Christian mind-set certainly has its roots in the materials of the
New Testament. Yet much of what is now identified with the
teachings of Jesus about morality and ethics in the Gospels is perhaps more accurately reflected in the later writings of the
Apostolic Fathers than with the contemporary teachings of early
first-century Judaism. It is almost impossible to know the complete extent to which the "novel" teachings of Jesus that are
known through our Gospels and were incorporated into the structure of the later church were actually first offered by Jesus of

Nazareth himself or, instead, were credited to him secondarily by the Christian authors who wrote the New Testament late in the first century.

One of the more interesting works within the Apostolic Fathers with respect to ethics is the *Epistle of Barnabas*. Beginning with a consideration of three instructions (or doctrines) that are related to humanity's hope for salvation, faith in a righteousness that leads to God's justice, and the joy that righteousness brings to Christian living, our author continues throughout the subsequent narrative to offer a number of essential traits that believers in Christ should possess. First and foremost among these traits is the quality of personal virtue, a human characteristic that must be supported by faith's helpers: fear, patience, endurance, and self-control. Each of these leads to purity. And it is purity of heart that all Christians need in order to withstand the wicked, twisted temptations of the Evil One, who is currently in power prior to the coming of the Lord. The author of *Barnabas* continues to explain how ancient Israel lost its own virtue in God's eyes through its aversion to faith, trusting in the external cult of sacrifices and turning away from the steadfast obedience to God's law that was the foundation of the covenant between the Lord and Judaism. Christians are subsequently warned not to make the same mistake, but to take the new covenant that God offers through the cross of Christ with great seriousness in order to secure their own salvation.

It is the combination of these four helpers of faith—fear, patience, endurance, self-control—that are of most interest to us here, since they recur in one form or another within most ethical considerations that appear throughout the Apostolic Fathers. Indeed, the author of *Barnabas* undoubtedly sees their importance as a primary motivation behind the addition of the "two ways" segment that is appended at the end of the text (chapters 18–20). The teaching of the "two ways" is actually dominated by such traits, qualities that advocate a respect for God and the importance of patient endurance in choosing the path that God would have Christians to follow, while avoiding the temptations of the Evil One that feature self-reliance and personal pride.

Discussion of the "two ways" naturally brings us to the text of the *Didache*, whose version of the motif features the Decalogue (Ten Commandments) at the core of its argument. Chapters 1–5, which preserve the "two ways," open with the ultimate definition of how Christians are to act as ethical beings. The followers of the way of life are enjoined to "love God who made you" first, and then "your neighbor as yourself." The roots of this teaching are easily traced to Deuteronomy 6:15 and Leviticus 19:18 and are featured on the lips of Jesus in the Gospels of Matthew, Mark, and Luke. Elsewhere, the rabbis of the first century made extensive use of each teaching, occasionally summarizing the saying from Leviticus as the précis of the Torah's lessons for humanity. The apostle Paul also offered this same teaching as an aspect of his advice to the church at Rome, perhaps reflecting common rabbinic teaching as much as the instruction of Jesus of Nazareth.

As further illustration of this love-of-God and love-of-neighbor commandment, the Didachist appends the teachings of the Decalogue as a guide to how such instruction is to be observed. As we observed in chapter 3, the reader is cautioned to avoid murder and adultery, theft and covetousness, and so forth. But in the midst of these great warnings one finds a compendium of lesser instructions designed to protect the reader from accidentally being led to even greater sins. Included here are warnings not to be sexually promiscuous or to be engaged in sorcery, not to commit perjury or to hold a grudge, not to become angry or to be conceited, not to grumble when giving alms, as well as instructions to make decisions without wavering, and so on. It seems that while the Didachist is fully aware of the "great sins" within the Judeo-Christian tradition, there is also a full-fledged consciousness that Christians are tempted with a never-ending series of lesser choices that may lead the followers of Christ down a path of destruction. The choice for lesser sins ultimately leads to a choice for greater iniquities it would seem.

As with *Barnabas*, we see that four fundamental traits of Christian ethical responsibility come into play in the scheme of the *Didache*: fear, patience, endurance, and self-control. First and foremost here is the trait of fear. This element is to be equated with fear and respect for the "God who made you." At the same time, it is to be found in the Christian's appreciation for the Law that God provides for humanity's guidance and salvation. Otherwise, the traits of patience, endurance, and self-control are prominently featured in the various instructions of *Didache* 1–5 that define how

Christians are to interact with one another. Indeed, instructions to avoid murder, adultery, pedophilia, promiscuity, theft, magic, sorcery, infanticide, covetousness, perjury, slander, grudges, lies, greed, hypocrisy, malicious schemes, anger, jealousy, lust, fornication, foul speech, idolatry, etc. are all based upon the basic premise that God's faithful people must be patient in their contact with others, must endure a variety of obvious personal injustices, and must exercise self-control in their social relationships. As the Didachist observes, all followers of the way of life must honor anyone who preaches God's Word and must treat that person as though he or she were the Lord. This concept of seeing other people in the guise of the Lord is not new, of course. One finds the teaching in the famous parable of the sheep and goats in Matthew 25. As is recorded on the lips of Jesus in that passage, to the extent that anyone feeds the hungry, gives drink to the thirsty, clothes the naked, visits the sick, or ministers to the imprisoned, they have done the same to Christ. And in this way, to love one's neighbor as oneself is in many respects a fulfillment of the demand that Christians likewise love the God who made them.

In the midst of this listing of ethical traits the Didachist emphasizes a command that is regularly seen throughout the writings of the Apostolic Fathers: "do not be double-minded or double-tongued." The early Christian concern for "double-mindedness" (hypocrisy) was widespread among the churches. It was probably a great temptation for many Christians of Jewish background to take a leap of faith into Christian theology while striving to maintain their traditional ties with Jewish traditions and teachings. The choice to break with ancestral norms was not made with ease. And the decision to turn away from relatives and familial customs ultimately led to the church's ouster from the synagogue communities in which early Christians first found safety for their beliefs. At the same time, the lack of structure that many early faith communities experienced as they attempted to answer questions that were related to their Jewish background, to the customs of non-Jews who were quickly overwhelming the rosters of the church by the end of the first century, to the nature of Jesus of Nazareth as the Messiah, to the issue of authority within the faith community, to options about doctrine and theology, and to liturgical practices and ethical choices undoubtedly led to numerous occasions in which individual Christians and entire congregations made important decisions with a large degree of hesitancy and uncertainty. These may have been choices for personal commitment to roles within the church or to the way that liturgy and worship were to be observed. But in any case, the answers to such questions were often offered through the lenses of a variety of options and rarely in the bold black and white selections that most people prefer.

Thus the Didachist, much as the author of *Barnabas*, warns Christians not to be double-minded. So too, the authors of *1 Clement* and the *Shepherd of Hermas* tender the same warning. According to *1 Clement*, Christians are not to be double-minded with respect to the nature of God the Father, for God is merciful and compassionate and lovingly bestows favors on those who approach with "singleness of mind." Drawing upon a scriptural source that remains uncertain, our author counsels the reader: "Wretched are the double-minded, those who doubt in their soul . . . " For *1 Clement* a mind that is pure in intention and without indecision is parallel to the will of God. And it is through this avenue that Christians can reassure themselves that they are living the type of life that Christ desires.

The *Shepherd* offers a similar idea about the nature of being double-minded. Early in the narrative, the church appears in the form of a woman and informs Hermas about a most important situation: "All those who are not double-minded will be cleansed of their sins." But somewhat later when we encounter Hermas in a state of wonderment at the many sights and instructions that he has received, his instructor, the Shepherd, asks him: "Why are you double-minded about the commandments that I gave to you?" It seems that the revelation of God's will is not so easily received in full faith. The Shepherd presently explains that those who are double-minded in their response to the salvation that God offers will eventually fall away and lose their lives. Ultimately, it is this very call to purity of heart that is brought to reality for Hermas, for it seems that both he and his entire household (the church?) are in peril of losing their salvation because of the double-mindedness that is to be found among them. The author of the *Shepherd* thus makes this theme a preeminent aspect of the writing's message for Christians. While there is little talk about the nature of theology or

105

the appropriate structure of church leadership and Christian evangelism, the *Shepherd* is clearly focused upon the need for common Christians to stop and reflect upon their lives in Christ. The necessity to live a life of single-minded purpose in response to the salvation that the Father has offered through the Son is of primary and immanent concern. Through true faith comes a worthy lifestyle. Through righteous living comes the salvation that God deems to be worthy. For Hermas and his family there is always time for repentance, as long as their hearts can be unified behind God's will for their lives.

This same theme of single-minded purpose seems to arise elsewhere within the Apostolic Fathers in writings that otherwise share little in common. One need only turn to the narrative of *2 Clement*, for example, to hear the advice, "Let us not be doubleminded, but patiently endure in hope so that we may also receive the reward." Here we once again find a vestige of themes that are heralded in *Barnabas*, specifically the call for patience and endurance. It is most instructive that the author of *2 Clement* offers these words within the context of a discussion about what it means to have a pure heart and, thus, to be righteous. Those who are double-minded and have doubt in their hearts have yielded to the tribulation and turmoil of their times. They have not held fast to the promise of God and thus will not enter into the kingdom of heaven. The Gospel of Matthew offers a collage of similar themes about the need for a righteousness that exists beyond that of the scribes and Pharisees. It offers hope for entry into the kingdom of heaven for those who can obtain that moral condition. In his own letter to the Philippians, Polycarp also comments upon the necessity of righteousness as an essential aspect of the Christian life. So too, it seems that *2 Clement* has incorporated this same theme into views about the coming kingdom, an idea that ultimately found a home in later Christian speculation with respect to the need for righteous living as a prerequisite for entry into the realm of God.

From *2 Clement* we may readily turn to the *Epistle to Diognetus*. This writing does not use the terminology of double-mindedness but clearly employs its related motif of hypocrisy. In this respect *Diognetus* is a noteworthy example of subsequent apologies that characterized the Christian literature of the late second and third centuries. Each of the great "apologists" of this period was concerned to defend the advent of the church against its presumed enemies, both in terms of theology and ethics. And a primary feature of this effort was the demonstration of Christianity's legitimacy in comparison with other faiths.

The author of *Diognetus* is particularly careful to demonstrate this feature of authenticity within the church. As is argued in the text, Christianity is distinct from paganism and Judaism in the very same way. For it seems that while both pagans and Jews are hypocritical in their actions, Christians are truly predisposed toward a faithful obedience to the one God of the world. Our author argues that pagans worship gods that have been made from common materials by their own hands. These so-called gods are fashioned from stone and wood, from bronze and silver, and from pottery. They must be protected from rust and decay and must be guarded against theft. It seems that the gods of such beliefs are completely dependent upon their makers! With respect to Judaism, their priests offer endless sacrifices of blood and fat as tokens of respect to the one true God. They keep sacred festivals and orient their calendars toward external rituals that are seen to be the fulfillment of God's commandments. But they have forgotten the call to ethical living that God's Torah also demands. While they seek to be true in their worship of God, they despise and hate their neighbors. Christians, on the other hand, are neither oriented toward the construction and protection of false gods nor toward the maintenance of annual rituals and festivals. Instead, the reader is informed that Christians may be distinguished by the ethical lifestyle that they lead. In many cases this results in persecution of members of the church both by pagans and Jews alike. But it is this faithful response to the call of Christ that helps Christians to persist in their actions, leading them to serve the world as concerned caretakers of humanity in their role as the body of Christ.

The witness of *Diognetus* is of inestimable value because of the link that it offers to the apologetic literature of succeeding decades. Its author manages to cull an early Christian concern for ethics and righteousness into a defense of what it means to be a part of the church. *Barnabas* and the *Didache* identify basic traits and characteristics that should be true to a valid Christian lifestyle, and *1–2 Clement* and the *Shepherd of Hermas* recognize that a pure heart of single-minded respect for God and humanity is essential for salvation. But the *Epistle of Diognetus* defines the context of these features—the moral life of Christian theology—as the primary element by which Christians may say who they are in distinction to other, competing faiths. There is no question that this focus upon Christian lifestyle, simple in form and conspicuously different from the more complex questions of theology and ecclesiology, came to dominate the faith life of ordinary Christians during the late patristic period. And it was upon this foundation of "right living" that the church came to control the social lives of its followers during the Byzantine Empire in the eastern Mediterranean world and the medieval era of Western Europe.

CHAPTER 6

Roots of the
Patristic Tradition

The majority of our discussion has been related to three primary areas of consideration: the nature of the materials that
have been preserved in the Apostolic Fathers, their relationship to other early Christian sources and traditions, and the people and ideas that had the most influence upon their composition.
This final chapter takes a decidedly different turn by virtue of its
focus upon the several ways in which the Apostolic Fathers have
influenced various authors and literary texts that arose in the centuries that followed. We have already mentioned certain ideas
from our collection that inspired later church leaders as, for example, the idea of penance that is found in the *Shepherd of Hermas* and
the concept of a three-tiered hierarchy of order that Ignatius of
Antioch advocates. But there is certainly much more to be taken
into account in this process. And we would be remiss to omit
some review of these elements.

Let us begin with a set of materials that has not received any
particular attention thus far, that is, the fragmentary remains of
the writings of the bishop Papias. As mentioned in chapter 1,
Papias is the author of a manuscript that circulated under the
title of the *Expositions of the Sayings of the Lord*. Though now lost
to history, later authors managed to preserve a few remnants from
his work. These texts offer an intriguing glimpse into certain

traditions and beliefs that circulated among the churches of the late first and early second centuries. But most importantly, they have greatly influenced popular beliefs about the nature of the apostles of Jesus and the origins of our New Testament Gospels.

Eusebius of Caesarea preserves specific observations by Papias about "the elders" of the church, including the original apostles and the evangelists. For example, Eusebius records that it was Papias who preserved the tradition that there were actually two tombs in Ephesus that held the remains of early Christian leaders who were named John, one of whom was John the son of Zebedee who traveled with Jesus, and the other was the prophet John who authored the book of Revelation. So too, Papias was a witness to the deeds of the apostle Philip, who lived with his daughters in the city of Hierapolis, the bishop's hometown.

But most important among these traditions are the words of Papias about the origins of two texts that are now associated with our New Testament Gospels.[1] In the first of these passages Eusebius has preserved these words from Papias:

> Mark, having been Peter's interpreter, accurately recorded all he remembered, though not in order, of anything that was said or done by Christ.

And in the second instance, Eusebius has recorded the following:

> Thus Matthew wrote the sayings in the Hebrew tongue, which everyone interpreted according to their ability.

The early church applied these comments to the two works that we now know as the Gospels of Mark and Matthew and assumed that these texts thus were authentic collections of sayings of Jesus based upon strict eyewitness accounts of the life and teachings of the man of Nazareth. With time, similar beliefs were applied to the Gospels of Luke and John. The impact of this perspective was that church leaders ultimately could appeal to such traditions as a rationale by which to include these particular Gospels into the New Testament while excluding other versions.

Modern biblical scholars have offered considerable challenges to such assumptions of the church that are based upon its interpretation of the words of Papias. Critics base their arguments upon evidence that there was some interaction among our Gospel authors to the extent that they may have had limited dependence upon one another's oral and literary sources and probably even upon some form of each other's actual Gospel texts. Further, scholars have observed that there is considerable indication that our Gospels are carefully constructed literary creations, not simply the unsystematic recording of random oral sources and memories. Finally, there seems to be little question that our Gospels were originally written in Greek and are not derived from translations of other ancient languages. The rising consensus of such observations about the compilation and creation of our New Testament Gospels has naturally been extremely painful for many modern Christians. But these views have ultimately been accepted into the teachings of the broader church on an official level, as is demonstrated by the Roman Catholic principle that the Gospels developed through three stages: the life and teachings of Jesus, a broad oral tradition, and a final writing down of the texts.[2] Most contemporary scholars acknowledge some form of this reality behind the creation of our Gospels. And yet there remains a resilient, pious conviction among many Christians that the Gospels preserve the eyewitness accounts of the apostles of Jesus who recorded their experiences of the Messiah with no divergence in perspective or faith. It is upon the words of Papias that such perspectives are quite typically based.

Since we have begun our review with the ancient city of Hierapolis in Asia Minor, it seems only appropriate to turn next to another important town in the same region, that is, Smyrna. This brings us to two writings in our collection, the letter of Polycarp to the Christians of Philippi in Greece and the *Martyrdom of Polycarp* that is addressed to the church of Philomelium in central Asia Minor.

With respect to Polycarp's epistle, there appears to be little from the correspondence that played an important role for later Christians. The issues that the bishop addresses in his letter are typical of early church concerns, including the question of how to live a righteous life, the importance of suitable leaders within the community, and what to do when confronted by those who abuse ecclesiastical authority. At the same time, however, it is clear from Polycarp's letter that he himself was a major player in early Christian circles. As we know from the *Martyrdom*, he lived to the advanced age of eighty-six. And as other writings attest, he traveled widely to Rome and throughout Asia Minor, having encountered the great Gnostic Marcion of Sinope whom he called "the firstborn of Satan." Several early patristic authors make mention of Polycarp as a revered pillar of sound doctrine and acceptable ecclesiastical practices, including Irenaeus and Tertullian, as well as Eusebius of Caesarea. Polycarp's authority and prestige were derived in large part from his role as a disciple of the apostle John. His memory continued to be revered by the church of Smyrna both through the *Martyrdom* and in the much later and highly fictionalized *A Life of Polycarp*. Indeed, to a large extent what little we actually know with certainty about the man Polycarp was often transferred by early Christian tradition to depict his somewhat older contemporary and friend, Ignatius of Antioch. Otherwise, we know little about Ignatius apart from his personal letters.

It is in the *Martyrdom* that we find materials from the tradition of Polycarp's life and character that have had the greatest impact upon later Christian thought and piety. Here we discover a most important transition in the way that early Christians viewed themselves as disciples of Christ. Prior to the *Martyrdom* the most prominent depiction of the death of an early follower of Jesus of Nazareth that was known from early Christian literature was the stoning of the deacon Stephen as preserved in Acts 7. Stephen's proclamation prior to his death, which is a recounting of the history of Israel until the crucifixion of Jesus, was undoubtedly a typical presentation of how the earliest church saw itself as the inheritor of God's covenant for humanity. But such a proclamation was typically Jewish in format and presentation. The death of Polycarp, on the other hand, is strictly depicted against the backdrop of Jesus of Nazareth's own arrest, trial, and crucifixion as known from the Gospels. And it was this particular imagery, symbols that were specifically in contrast to Judaism's rejection of the church, that came to have the greatest appeal for early Christians.

Indeed, the ancient church's vision of the perfect disciple who sacrificed everything for faith became a popular reality for later Christians who found themselves living during times of persecution throughout the Roman Empire. As observed in our discussion above, the structure of the *Martyrdom of Polycarp*, whose narrative offers the noble death of a pious Christian leader in bold imitation of the crucifixion of Christ on behalf of the church, became the typical pattern by which subsequent martyrdoms were often portrayed. This literary imitation is easily seen in such works as *The Martyrdom of Perpetua and Felicitas* from the beginning of the third century, the fourth-century *Acts of Phileas*, and the fifth-century *Acts of the Scillitan Martyrs*. But elements of the pattern are clearly evident throughout the large corpus of other martyrologies that have been preserved well into the medieval period.

Perhaps the most intriguing element of the tradition of Polycarp is the inspiration that his demise provided for numerous Christians who came to see a righteous death as the most important aspect of religious faith. Many of the church's faithful followers soon pursued their own deaths at the hands of civil authorities, turning themselves over as willing sacrifices for God's kingdom. By the third century, bishops throughout the Mediterranean world began to legislate against such unbridled enthusiasm among their parishioners in an effort to stem the tide of needless sacrifice that had managed to decimate many local church communities. As they observed, living for Christ was certainly as important as dying for him!

We proceed to the bishop Ignatius, whose letters have provided numerous images for later church leaders. The actual trial and execution of Ignatius remains unknown, though a much later account was recorded posthumously in the *Martyrdom of Ignatius*, a work that scholars believe to be highly fictitious and undoubtedly influenced to some extent by the account of the *Martyrdom of Polycarp*. Otherwise, the letters that Ignatius penned along his way to Rome have left a cornucopia of images that the pious tradition of church history has incorporated into its broader understanding of what it means to be a devoted servant of Christ.

Most important among these images is the Ignatian belief that the bishop, representing the presence of God within each Christian community, must provide complete approval for all elements of the liturgical and administrative life of the church. It is through the bishop alone that the church finds its true meaning. Thus Ignatius insists that all Christians must be in harmony with the will of the bishop, much like the strings of a harp when they are in perfect tune. This image of harmonious music appears at various points throughout his letters. For example, in the same way that the heavens are constructed to produce "the music of the spheres," so too must the unified voices of the church confess their faith in Christ as an earthly reflection of that heavenly reality. For Ignatius, Christian harmony is a reflection of the presence of God among those people who seek to form the body of Christ. And the focus of that harmony must necessarily be directed toward the bishop, around whom all decisions should be made and through whom all actions should be conducted.

Numerous patristic authors made use of the Ignatian tradition, including Irenaeus, Origen, Eusebius of Caesarea, Athanasius, and Jerome. In most cases these theologians were interested in the level of devotion and piety that the bishop had demonstrated in his writings. They made use of his tendency to utilize creeds as a means by which to combat divergent and troublesome theologies. This is particularly evident in the writings of the great "heresiologists" of the late third and fourth centuries, church leaders who were particularly concerned that Christians adhere to a unified theology that recognized the threefold nature of the triune God, the integrity of the institutional church, and the sacramental value of a shared liturgy. They were also impressed with his understanding of a single "catholic" (universal) church as distinct from competing faiths that had claimed the authority of Christ for their own beliefs. This insistence upon a sole genuine form of the church's faith was not new to Christian thinkers, of course. Even the New Testament demonstrates the conflict between the theological convictions of its writers, such as the apostle Paul and the author of 1–3 John, and those whom they condemned as resistant to their version of the "good news" message. But with Ignatius there is clearly a move to associate a single doctrinal position with specific church communities. It is Ignatius himself, at least according to our literary sources, who offers a means by which to associate a so-called "rule of faith" with a specific institutional tradition. And so it is that modern ecclesiastical traditions have come to define their identity according to one form or another of such faith confessions.

Much like Polycarp after him, Ignatius ultimately came to represent the ultimate figure of Christian devotion. His letters suggest that he was a fervent follower of Christ who was less concerned for his own life than for the harmonious existence of the

Christians that he served as pastor and of those whom he encountered along his way to Rome. The image of piety that Ignatius inspires led his followers to produce a small number of additional epistles in his name, undoubtedly to answer a variety of questions about his ideas and the influence of his authority among other church leaders that are not addressed in his original correspondence. There is no question that what he left for us in terms of creeds, sound doctrine, church structure, and unwavering devotion in the face of certain persecution has become a standard by which later Christians have come to measure their own faith and allegiance to the figure of Christ. And in this regard, if for no other reason, Ignatius has remained a pivotal figure of the tradition while his ideas have influenced the tide of doctrinal development and institutional structure.

From Ignatius we move to the text of *1 Clement*, a work that engages many of the same themes. The occasion for the writing of this letter naturally leads us to the assumption that its text was valued and preserved among the manuscripts collected by the church at Corinth. After all, it was that community's request for assistance from the church at Rome that prompted the production of the epistle in the first place. And as observed in chapter 1 above, its very existence undoubtedly led to the title that we now apply to the homily of *2 Clement* that was used by that same Corinthian church. It is only natural to assume that *1 Clement* was widely known and employed by Christians in the region.

A most intriguing element of the letter is the fact that it was also broadly respected among scattered church theologians outside of Greece. Its materials are reflected in the writings of Irenaeus and Tertullian, for example, and also by Eusebius of Caesarea. And in Alexandria, the location of the renowned ancient Alexandrian Library, it found a home within the writings of certain leaders of the catechetical school there, Clement of Alexandria and Origen. Within the city of Rome there is evidence that the great scholar Jerome knew the letter as well. But interestingly, it does not seem to have been used by Hippolytus. Perhaps the greatest testimony to the fame of the work may be derived from its presence in the famous fifth-century New Testament manuscript that is now known as *Codex Alexandrinus*, one of the early church's greatest biblical documents. The presence of *1 Clement* within this collection certainly suggests that it was held with a reverence that the early church reserved primarily for works of scripture.

The primary value of *1 Clement* for later Christian authors may be found in its insistence upon the need for order and harmony within the church. Much like the metaphor of musical harmony that Ignatius employs in his own writings, *1 Clement* appeals to the divine directions that only God can give to creation. As stated by the author, the heavens follow the course that God directs: the day follows the night, the sun and moon and stars move along their assigned paths, the earth produces in its season. Indeed, "all of these have been ordered to act in peace and harmony by the Creator and Lord of the universe."[3] It was this very premise that came to dominate the thinking of later patristic authors and that ultimately guided theologians and bishops alike to divide the Mediterranean world into dominant regions of church power, namely, the influential cities of Rome, Alexandria, Antioch, and Constantinople.

Of particular interest in this process is the final prayer that the author of *1 Clement* offers toward the end of the text in chapters 59–61. Here we find petitions to the Creator of the universe to preserve the elect, to raise those who have fallen, to judge the righteous, and to guard those who are weak. Intermingled with these petitions is language that recognizes the omnipotent nature of God as ruler of all creation. God is called the primal source of all things, highest of the high and most holy of the holy, creator and guardian of every spirit, marvelous in strength and majesty, king of the ages, and heavenly master. It is easy to observe that such traits form the very essence of how the church ultimately came to define the nature of God the Father: Eternal King, Creator of the Universe, and Lord of all Power. And the heart of such language was soon folded into the general faith confessions of the church, finding its earthly expression in the holy power of earthly bishops as the representatives of the presence of God.

It is particularly instructive that by the Middle Ages the text of *1 Clement* had basically disappeared from the literature of the church. At the same time, however, the name of the supposed author of the text, Clement of Rome, gained a certain reverence within ecclesiastical circles as an early pope of the Roman Catholic tradition. To some extent this suggests that, once the church of

Rome had acquired the authority and security that a text like *1 Clement* offered, there was no longer any particular need for the writing itself.

It seems prudent to move to another Roman text at this juncture, the *Shepherd of Hermas*, whose ultimate function within the church lies closely parallel to that of *1 Clement*. A copy of the *Shepherd* has been preserved in yet another famous early Christian biblical manuscript, the fourth-century *Codex Sinaiticus*. As with the case of *1 Clement*, this suggests that its value was widely recognized by early Christians. Further, the *Shepherd* was known and used by a variety of patristic authors, including Irenaeus and Tertullian, Clement and Origen in Egypt, Hippolytus, Cyprian, Eusebius of Caesarea, Athanasius, Ambrose, Jerome, Augustine, and Cassian.

These writers viewed the text quite favorably, though sometimes with hesitancy. In many instances the *Shepherd* became a text of debate, since it was so heavily focused upon the role of the Holy Spirit in Christian life. This is nowhere more evident than with the great Montanist controversies of the late second and third centuries, a period when widespread concern for the role of the Spirit in contemporary Christian prophecy gained prominence among laity and clergy alike. As is otherwise evident from a survey of Christian literature from the second century, discussions of the role of the Holy Spirit, especially with respect to prayer in the church, was not widely found. Because these years occurred somewhat prior to the church's doctrinal decisions about the role of the Spirit within the godhead of the Trinity, the place of the Spirit in daily Christian living and weekly liturgical rituals was highly speculative. Those Christians whose faith life and personal theology were too highly dependent upon the Spirit often came into conflict with the leadership of the church, which was naturally quite suspicious of a spiritual movement that could not be so easily controlled. The result was that many pious Christians found themselves separated from the evolving position of the institutional hierarchy as it struggled to establish its authority among local churches. And the views of the *Shepherd* on the nature of the Spirit sometimes became the focus of such discussions.

Of course, the *Shepherd* was also influential among patristic authors for the same reason that *1 Clement* became popular, that is, for its insistence upon the authority of the church as a governing agent of individual Christian faith. In many respects this appears to be a primary concern behind the narrative of the text, whose structure combines three collections of visions, commandments, and parables into a collage of instructions about an individual's responsibility to the larger church body. The continuing problem of the narrative's hero, Hermas, is that he stands as a loner within the tradition. He tends to think for himself and to respond to situations in life without consideration for the teachings of the church. As a result the reader comes to see that Hermas needs the guidance of "mother church" and the Shepherd. The first of these characters, depicted as a woman at different stages of life, provides the stability of an ancient tradition out of which the church had developed, including the witness of Judaism's patriarchs, the apostles and prophets, and the continuous lineage of apostolic authority that was to be found among the bishops and presbyters. The second character, the Shepherd, provides the essential teachings and instructions that a Christian needs in order to live a righteous lifestyle in the eyes of God. Hence, the *Shepherd* offers a two-pronged avenue by which early Christians could follow suitable lives according to the evolving tradition of the institutional church.

There are many ways in which the narrative and tenor of the *Shepherd* came to dominate the later theological perspective of late patristic and medieval theologians. Its vision of the church as a tower, built upon a solid rock, fashioned from stones that are suitable in the eyes of God, ultimately came to describe what the medieval church expected from its own parishioners. The durability of the institutional church, at least as seen within the model that the *Shepherd* provides, ultimately found its popular expression in the morality plays of the Middle Ages. On another level, the growing power of the Roman papacy learned to relish this image of strength and durability that was captured by the author of the *Shepherd*. It was an image that provided comfort for Christians during the centuries of threat that arose with the demise of the Roman Empire under the pressure of invasion by Germanic tribes.

This motif of "reassurance" that tends to dominate the narrative of the *Shepherd* can also be discovered throughout the text of *2 Clement*. As observed above, the author of *2 Clement* begins with the assertion that Christians must think of Christ as they think of God, that is, as the judge of the living and the dead. But further, to live responsibly for Christ also means to exist as the living body of Christ in the world, in other words, as the church. This church was created in the Spirit of God even before the heavens were formed. And now it dwells within the flesh of those who honor the Lord. This is an interesting evolution of several themes that the *Shepherd* had already raised: the role of the Spirit, the eternal nature of the church, and the individual Christian's responsibility to maintain a life of devoted faith and ethical purity. But in the case of *2 Clement*, our author has combined these elements into a theological viewpoint that is fashioned upon biblical foundations. Here the place of the Spirit within the life of the Christian comes through a believer's recognition that having faith in Christ brings one into the structure of the living church and, hence, into the presence of the Spirit.

For *2 Clement*, the insistence upon an ethical lifestyle serves as the core theme of the text. The reader is told that it is essential to be obedient to the commands of Christ and, thus, to the teachings of the church. All Christians, people who are merely sojourners in this world, can indicate such obedience through their actions, keeping their baptisms pure and unblemished, continuously competing with temptation in order to achieve the heavenly reward, and accepting the need for repentance. The motivation for such actions comes through a fear of the coming day of God's judgment, a time when those who have taught falsely, have been double-minded, and have blasphemed the name of the Lord will be excluded from the spiritual church and from the resurrection of God's faithful.

It has been observed that *2 Clement*, which is considered by many scholars to be our oldest complete Christian homily, could easily be preached among and understood by modern Christians. It clearly had the respect of the early church by virtue of its presence in the *Codex Alexandrinus*, one of our primary sources for the text of *1 Clement* as well. But outside of this great biblical manuscript, there does not seem to be much evidence to suggest that our homily circulated widely among important patristic writers. Unlike either *1 Clement* or the *Shepherd*, later authors, including the great theologians of Alexandria in Egypt who otherwise seem to have been aware of many ancient Christian manuscripts, do not employ the text of *2 Clement*.

This lack of knowledge about *2 Clement* among the authors of the patristic church also seems to hold true for another writing from the Apostolic Fathers, the *Epistle to Diognetus*. Only Clement of Alexandria indicates any knowledge of *Diognetus*, unless we accept the fragmentary text of the *Apology of Quadratus* that was preserved by Eusebius of Caesarea[4] to be an authentic reference to some portion of the work.

In the case of *Diognetus*, however, there seems to be a good explanation for why the text was not more widely employed among patristic authors. The text of *Diognetus* is unique within the Apostolic Fathers as an apology. It is a defense of the church and the Christian faith against those who charged that Christianity was a late, and therefore spurious, religion that had no value when compared to the more ancient teachings of paganism or the glorious traditions of Judaism. But *Diognetus* is a brief work and does not compare well with longer and better-illustrated apologies that would have been preferred by later Christian theologians and preachers. One might include here the apologies of Justin Martyr, Tertullian, Apollinaris of Hierapolis, Melito of Sardis, Theophilus of Antioch, and Tatian. A second consideration is that *Diognetus* is one of our more recent writings within the Apostolic Fathers, perhaps having been composed toward the end of the second century. One would not necessarily expect such a text to have gained a wide circulation among patristic authors who wrote only a short time later. Finally, there is little within the text of *Diognetus* that might be considered as a new idea for the great thinkers of the church. Its author, while clever in the presentation of themes and in the vision of Christianity's role within the world, actually offers little that cannot be found elsewhere.

Ultimately *Diognetus* does not seem to have been widely used either by patristic authors or medieval writers. This is perhaps best illustrated by the fact that no copy of the text survives today. Our complete knowledge of the work derives from an individual Greek manuscript that was preserved among the writings of Justin Martyr, itself ultimately destroyed by fire.

Two final texts remain for consideration: the *Epistle of Barnabas* and the *Didache*. Each of these has had a particularly interesting influence upon later Christian writers, but for different reasons. In the case of *Barnabas*, the influence may be seen in the idea of Christian knowledge that the author endorses. In the situation of the *Didache*, it is found in the format for ethical training that later writers adopted and adapted for their own purposes.

We turn first to *Barnabas*. As observed above, the predominant themes of the author of *Barnabas* include three basic teachings of faith, righteousness, and joy. These teachings, or doctrines, are not offered as ends unto themselves, however, but are depicted as elements of a special knowledge for which all Christians should seek. If we can accept the region of Egypt (perhaps even Alexandria more specifically) as the location in which *Barnabas* was written, then this focus upon "knowledge" becomes especially important. For it was primarily in Egypt (and secondarily in Syria) that a concern for Christian knowledge came into prominence within the early church. At its most extreme level of interpretation, the special knowledge that only "true" Christians were believed to possess was seen as the basis for God's salvation and, hence, as the ultimate goal for which believers in Christ should strive. This particular doctrine came to characterize the so-called Gnostic church that eventually managed to spread throughout the Mediterranean world. But the apex of this movement remained within the churches of Egypt and Syria.

This is not to assert that either the text of *Barnabas* or its author was Gnostic. Indeed, there is little in our writing to suggest that its theology was principally dependent upon some special knowledge for salvation that lies beyond any other facet of Christian theology, including elements such as faith, hope, and love as listed by the apostle Paul in 1 Corinthians 13. One might argue instead that *Barnabas* represents merely the fertile background of speculation about the role of special Christian knowledge that became a basis of ethical Christian living. On the one hand, this knowledge entails a duty to live the moral existence of someone who is obedient to Christ as the Savior. On the other hand, such knowledge demands that each believer pursue some further and deeper understanding of what it means to be a part of the kingdom of God in both a theological and spiritual sense. Such emphases continued to develop within the church of Alexandria through two noted leaders of the local catechetical school that operated within

121

the city, Clement and Origen. One would naturally expect that both of these men would indicate some knowledge of *Barnabas* in their writings. And so they do! Of course, other patristic authors outside of Egypt also seem to have known *Barnabas*, including Tertullian, Jerome, and Eusebius of Caesarea. But the use of *Barnabas*, with its theological focus upon knowledge as an essential resource of Christian development, is particularly intriguing among Alexandrian writers, since it suggests that the text lay at the foundation of what was to become a major theological movement within the region. Furthermore, it is especially important that *Barnabas*, much like the *Shepherd of Hermas*, appears within the *Codex Sinaiticus*. This fact stands as further testimony to the importance of the text within the broader Egyptian church where that codex was produced. The ideas of knowledge that the author of *Barnabas* endorses seem to have gained a wide acceptance among a number of Christians, at least in the southeastern region of the Mediterranean world.

Finally, we turn to the text of the *Didache*, whose materials and traditions have had a significant impact upon later patristic thinkers. Unlike *Barnabas*, however, the *Didache* does not represent the foundations of an early Christian tradition that ultimately came to dominate any particular school of ancient theology. Instead, it seems that it was the ethical teachings of the *Didache*, specifically the "two ways" material, that attracted the interest of later ecclesiastical authors.

Let us recall that the *Didache* is basically composed of two primary groupings of texts. The first group (found in chapters 1–6) is composed of the "two ways" material that circulated widely among Jews and Christians alike. As illustrated above, vestiges of this teaching may be found in Deuteronomy, Sirach, the Gospel of Matthew, the Dead Sea Scrolls, and *Barnabas*, to name but a few sources. The manuscript tradition behind the *Didache* itself suggests a special emphasis upon this teaching, since our single Latin witness to the *Didache* preserves the "two ways" section only, indicating that it circulated without the rest of the text at some point in its early literary history. The second group of materials (found in chapters 7–16) is composed primarily of liturgical instructions and directions for the administration of a church community. These texts focus upon directives for baptism, eating rituals, prayer, the role of apostles and prophets within the community, the nature of worthy bishops and deacons, observance of the Lord's Day, and warnings about the end times. Unlike the first part of the text, there is little concern for ethical instruction here. Instead, these materials maintain a concerted focus upon the regulation of community life.

Many scholars who have investigated the *Didache* have labeled the text as a "church order," or an ecclesiastical handbook for the regulation of community activities, especially with respect to liturgical and ecclesiastical concerns. And this may actually be how the patristic church saw the text, since it was variously incorporated into later texts that served a similar purpose. Most important among these later writings is the widely used, fourth-century *Apostolic Constitutions*, a lengthy writing in which the materials of the *Didache* serve as the framework for Book 7. So too, we must include Section 52 of the church manual known as the *Apostolic Church Order*, whose author made extensive use of the *Didache*. Texts such as these were designed by church leaders to offer instruction for deacons and presbyters, as well as for laity who served important functions within church communities. It is clear they recognized the value that our text held for the development of ecclesiastical offices as the institutional church shaped itself into a significant religious and cultural power in the late Roman Empire.

But beyond the patristic period we discover it was the "two ways" portion of the *Didache* that held the most interest for leaders within the church. And, even at that, these materials were employed primarily within esoteric writings that were not utilized within the mainline tradition. For example, the Arabic *Life of Shenoute*, which is an account of the life and teachings of the desert monk Shenoute of Atripe from the fifth century, contains significant portions of the "two ways" tradition among the teachings of this early monastic father. And the slightly later *Rule of Benedict*, which is based upon the early sixth-century teachings of the founder of the Benedictine monastery system, Benedict of Nursia, reveals a great dependence upon the "two ways" tradition, particularly in Section 4 of the work. But in these works it is not the tradition itself that is highlighted but, instead, the teachings of the famous leader who is featured by the author. The instructions of the "two ways" have simply been interwoven throughout those teachings as a secondary portion of the narrative.

In summary, it is easy to find that the individual writings of the Apostolic Fathers had a significant impact upon later writers of the patristic period and, in some cases, even upon later thinkers of the church. Today there are certain segments of our collection that are employed for specific purposes by contemporary Christian leaders. For example, arguments against abortion among modern church leaders ultimately find little specific support within biblical literature apart from the prohibition against taking human life in general. But in the Apostolic Fathers, there are two specific prohibitions in *Barnabas* and the *Didache* that ban such practices among early Christians.[5] And most Christians who have any familiarity with the early history of the church beyond the first century are nominally aware of the faith witness that both Ignatius and Polycarp offered to the tradition by virtue of their resilience in the face of persecution and death. It was leaders such as these who provided the framework by which subsequent bishops, martyrs, teachers, and theologians provided both spiritual and theological inspiration for their followers during times of hardship. The call of *1–2 Clement* and the *Shepherd of Hermas* for unity, harmony, and order within the church soon caught the ear of individual faith communities who struggled with the problems of division and factionalism within their midst. It was to just such texts that church historians like Eusebius of Caesarea and Sozomen could appeal for their arguments on behalf of apostolic succession and historical continuity. Indeed, the insights of the Apostolic Fathers served them well.

Conclusions

The collected writings of the early church that are now classified as the Apostolic Fathers unfortunately remain a complete mystery to most Christians. And yet, these texts represent a pivotal moment in the history of Christianity that ultimately helped to shape the way in which modern Christians have come to understand who they are as followers of Jesus of Nazareth. The Apostolic Fathers witness to the important transition that the church made as it evolved beyond the roots of its fledgling New Testament beliefs into an institution of faith confessions, liturgical rituals, ecclesiastical regulations, and ethical norms. What is preserved within these documents is a firsthand vision of how that transition was best accomplished, at least from the perspective of scattered church leaders as they encountered the problems of being a Christian in a culture that was often hostile to their presence.

Perhaps the greatest beauty of these works may be found in the multiple images of the ancient church that the assembled writings offer as a collective voice. Here we find the struggles of the Syrian bishop Ignatius who, threatened with certain torture and death, continues to preach against false doctrines and in favor of churches whose life of faith is unified under the leadership of worthy bishops, presbyters, and deacons. So too, we see a friend of his, the bishop Polycarp from Asia Minor, who reinforces these same themes of doctrinal integrity and ecclesiastical order as a further witness to the needs of the developing church in the second century. His own followers choose to record his ultimate witness of faith, now preserved in the account of his martyrdom at the hands of the Roman government. And when the church in Corinth encounters similar problems with respect to order within the body of Christ, they appeal to the church at Rome for advice and assistance, thus providing the occasion for the writing of *1 Clement*. The vision of Roman order that this epistle provides is clearly supplemented by a second Roman text, the *Shepherd of Hermas*, whose focus upon the requirements of an ethical lifestyle and purity of heart was a major concern of the evolving church. Similar considerations are paralleled in two other texts, the *Didache* and *Barnabas*, writings that offer quite specific ways by which to understand how Christians should live their daily lives and the importance of grasping the covenant that God offers for salvation. Yet, as the author of *2 Clement* observes, the key to the entire process is to be found in the role that Christ fulfills as the savior of humanity. The presence of Christ within the lives of those who follow him should be evident to all who witness the church at work in the world, at least according to the argument of the *Epistle to Diognetus*. And the foundation for understanding that witness may be discovered in the testimony of those who have guided the church since its inception during the ministry of Jesus of Nazareth, as argued from the fragmentary traditions that are preserved by the bishop Papias.

The Apostolic Fathers offer a broad gathering of different visions and diverse voices from around the ancient Mediterranean world, each of which attests to the early Christian experience within its own sphere of influence. Their understanding of the evolving church was shaped in part by the same realities that challenged the apostle Paul and the evangelists who wrote our New Testament Gospels: the need to identify what it meant to be a Christian beyond the theological foundation and ritual limitations of Judaism, the need to share a faith experience that was both unique to each believer and somehow common to other Christians, and the need to define the role of the church within a hostile culture of competing religions and cults. Yet their views were also shaped by the realization that the existence of the church was ultimately going to be fashioned by long-term inter-

126

ests: the need to establish orderly methods by which to select leaders for each faith community, the need to determine which doctrinal views were acceptable and which lay outside of the boundaries of theological tolerance, and the need to define the parameters of a suitable ethical lifestyle that would help Christians to live and work as active members of the body of Christ within the world.

Included among these materials are ideas and traditions that spanned the ancient world from Egypt to Greece, and from Asia Minor to Rome. Preserved here are thoughts and customs that were widely accepted by Christians and faith communities in various locations. The texts themselves were often revered in the same light as other writings that eventually became recognized as works of scripture. This is evident from the inclusion of works like *1–2 Clement*, the *Shepherd of Hermas*, and *Barnabas* within the ancient codices that many church communities considered to be authoritative for liturgical purposes and devotional study. And even the Alexandrian bishop Athanasius, when he offered the list of writings that he considered to be scriptural in nature (a list that basically forms the same canonical boundaries that are observed by most Christian traditions to this day), included most of our texts as useful for instruction and worthy of respect, if not ultimately essential as scripture.

The modern practice by which scholars group our writings into a single collection of literature from the early church under the designation of the Apostolic Fathers indicates that these texts stood out from among the vast variety of competing writings that were known by Christians in the late first and second centuries. Some of those competitors were ultimately classified as scripture by the church, and hence were preserved as an integral part of the life and work of Christian tradition. The criteria by which such texts were judged included the apostolic origins of their sources, the wide usage that they enjoyed among different churches, the appropriate nature of the theology that their authors endorsed, and their suitability for preaching, teaching, and devotion. Of course, the church rejected many other works according to these same criteria. Writings such as the *Gospel of Thomas* and the *Gospel of Truth*, to name but a few, were ultimately discarded from the mainline tradition, most likely because they were not considered

127

to support an appropriate theology. The popular *Acts of Paul and Thecla* was abandoned because of its lack of apostolic authority. It is all the more impressive, therefore, that the writings that form our Apostolic Fathers, while not ultimately accepted into the New Testament by subsequent church tradition, were preserved within church communities and valued for their contributions to questions of theology and ecclesiastical practice. They were not canonized, but neither were they rejected. In this way we might argue with some justification that, despite the fact that these writings derive from a variety of different authors and geographical settings, they do indeed stand as a unified corpus of writings that depict a genuine faith among early Christians.

One of the more valuable aspects of the Apostolic Fathers for modern Christians is the avenue that they provide for a better understanding of other texts. As an example, despite the letters that remain in the New Testament from Paul's correspondence with the church in Corinth, we would have an infinitely poorer understanding of that community in later decades without the text of *1 Clement* and, perhaps, *2 Clement*. By the same token, we are familiar with the church in Rome from Paul's letter to that community. But Paul presumably had never visited the church there and wrote primarily from his limited impression of what it must be like. Texts such as *1 Clement* and the *Shepherd* help to provide a broader context of the issues and perspectives that the Roman church supported in the years after Paul's ministry brought him to the city. The letter of Ignatius to the church in Rome also offers some additional insight into the social and civic powers that the local community may have held, since Ignatius emphatically pleaded that such leverage not be applied on his behalf. We may also point to Polycarp's letter to the Philippians as a helpful tool in coming to understand the concerns of the church of Philippi in the second century, as well as the situation of the bishop's home community in Smyrna. Other texts such as *Barnabas*, the *Didache*, *2 Clement*, and *Diognetus* do not offer such a clear glimpse into the life of faith of any specifically named church community. But their contribution to the early church's context should not be dismissed, since they provide broad strokes by which to understand ideas and trends within the church that have often disappeared over the centuries. And to the extent that these particular texts can be identified with individual faith communities, even if simply by speculation, they may add potential pieces toward a reconstruction of the early church that otherwise remains incomplete.

In the final analysis it would be a gross overstatement to claim that the Apostolic Fathers offer an answer to all of our modern questions about the earliest development of the church after the New Testament period. At the same time, however, it is certainly fair to say that our helpful knowledge of these materials enables us to better understand how the views of biblical authors came to fruition in the subsequent years of Christianity's historical evolution. The concerns of New Testament authors were certainly raised and addressed in their day. But it often appears that they were rarely resolved. Warnings against false prophets and errant teachings, calls for a life of righteous living and ethical norms, and subtle maneuvers for ecclesiastical primacy and church power among biblical authors were continued well beyond the world of first-century Christian communities. Indeed, such issues were adopted by those who inherited the traditions of the earliest church leaders and were adapted to meet the needs of devoted followers of Christ who quickly found themselves being transformed from a pious, messianic Jewish sect into a full-fledged religious movement. It was a movement that eventually managed to reach out to the Mediterranean world with a message that was uniquely its own.

The Apostolic Fathers provide a key insight into this process of religious evolution and the nature of the transmission of Christian faith. For while those modern Christians who would claim that there was no dissension among first-century believers are clearly ignorant about the strife that lies behind the narrative of the books of Acts and Revelation, the letters of Paul to Corinth and Galatia, the letters of 1–3 John, 2 Peter, and Jude, the testimony of the Apostolic Fathers insists that the basic Christian faith that our biblical authors experienced and preached continued to inspire the next generation of Christians who soon produced our writings. Their vision of what it meant to be a Christian—the need for an ethical lifestyle, the urgency of living in the kingdom of God, the importance of sound doctrine and correct liturgy, the affirmation of the church as an eternal and solid expression of Christ at work in the world—served to inspire the imagery and theology of later patristic writers who found themselves in conflict with Roman culture, competing religious views, and alternative lifestyles that pushed beyond the boundaries of what they considered to be religious decency.

The Apostolic Fathers truly stand at a pivotal point in the earliest history of the rise of Christian theology and institutional structure. The authors of each text within that collection of literature were worthy participants in the development of individual churches, communities of faith that were forced to define what it meant to live as a Christian in a time of struggle and hardship. Their witness to belief and doctrine, their preservation of resilient biblical traditions, and their pastoral application of faith, hope, and love in the establishment of a working Christian environment provided the solid foundation upon which later theologians and ecclesiastical leaders could construct the edifices of subsequent stages of church development. For those who are ignorant of the Apostolic Fathers, there might seem to be some significant confusion about how the faith of New Testament Christianity came to be expressed in the later evolution of the church. But for those who have read these texts and learned from their lessons, the useful light of that knowledge will surely help to clarify the mysteries of the ancient Christian experience.

Notes

1. The Collected Writings

1. See Acts 4:32-37; 9:26-30; 11:19-30; 12:25; 13:1-12, 42-52; 14:8-20; 15:1-41; 1 Cor 9:6; Gal 2:1-14; Col 4:10.

2. And as some scholars would argue, even this manuscript may be missing a few lines from its conclusion.

3. The death of Ignatius is recounted in a work known as the *Martyrium Ignatii*, which is almost certainly a secondary reminiscence of the event that was designed to inspire the faith of later Christians.

4. Some collections of the letters of Ignatius include additional correspondence, but scholars have generally rejected these works as spurious. Included here is a letter each to the churches in Tarsus, Antioch, and Philippi, as well as letters to the deacon Hero of Antioch, Mary of Cassobelae, and two letters to the presbyter John. Also included is a letter from Mary of Cassobelae to Ignatius.

5. Parallel examples in the New Testament may be found in 1–2 Cor (possibly four letters combined) and Phil (possibly two or three letters combined).

6. Eusebius, *Eccl. Hist.* 4.3.1-2.

2. People and Places

1. See Acts 9:1-25; 22:4-16; 26:9-18.

2. For example, he finds Christians already present in Syrian Antioch (Acts 11:19-26) and Ephesus (Acts 19:1-7).

3. As seen in Gal 1:15-18.

131

4. Acts 28:13-14.

5. *Acts Pet.* 6 (from the Latin "Vercelli Acts").

6. Tertullian, *Praescr.* 32.

7. Herm. *Vis.* 2.4.3.

8. See Acts 17:1-15.

9. Eusebius, *Eccl. Hist.* 4.26.10.

10. Rom 16:1.

11. As seen in Titus 3:12; cf. 2 Tim 4:10.

12. Phil 4:16.

13. Ign. *Phld.* 3.1.

3: Connections to Scripture

1. At the same time, however, Ignatius makes a single reference to "the archives" in his letter to the Philadelphians (see 8.2), which most scholars understand to be the Old Testament. He states: "For I heard some people say, 'If I do not find it in the archives, I do not believe it in the gospel.'" We have seen above that the Philadelphians were in constant conflict with the synagogue, which would indeed seem to support the idea of this association of archives with Jewish scriptures. At the same time, of course, this does not necessarily mean that Ignatius himself was particularly familiar with the contents of the collection.

2. This idea was first offered by Hans von Campenhausen in the twentieth century.

3. See *Did.* 8.

4. See *Did.* 7.

5. Ign. *Eph.* 18.

6. Ign. *Trall.* 6.

7. Ign. *Magn.* 8.

4. Theological Ideas

1. Matt 28:19 (cf. 2 Cor 13:14). 1 John 5:7 also contains a similar Trinitarian formula in some translations of the epistle, but most scholars now believe the phrase to represent a late insertion into the text.

2. Gen 1:26, 28 (see *Barn.* 6.12).

3. *1 Clem.* 16.

4. *1 Clem.* 36.1.

5. *Did.* 7.1, 3. Curiously, the Didachist uses the Trinitarian formula in association with baptism, much like it is found in Matthew.

6. *Eph.* 7.2 and *Trall.* 9.1-2 respectively.

7. *Phil.* 7.1.

5. Structures of the Ancient Church

1. Herm. *Mand.* 4.1.8.
2. *Eph.* 18.2.

6. Roots of the Patristic Tradition

1. Eusebius, *Eccl. Hist.* 3.39.
2. Catechism of the Catholic Church §126.
3. *1 Clement* 20.
4. Eusebius, *Eccl. Hist.* 4.3.1-2.
5. See, e.g., *Catechism of the Catholic Church* §2271, whose note refers to *Barn.* 19.5 and *Did.* 2.2. Also included here is a reference to the author of *Diognetus,* who observes that Christians do not "expose their offspring" as a form of child euthanasia (see *Diog.* 5.6).